Defending the Fringe

The Johns Hopkins Foreign Policy Institute (FPI) was founded in 1980 and serves as the research center for the School of Advanced International Studies (SAIS) in Washington, D.C. The FPI is a meeting place for SAIS faculty members and students as well as for government analysts, policymakers, diplomats, journalists, business leaders, and other specialists in international affairs. In addition to conducting research on policy-related international issues, the FPI sponsors conferences, seminars, and roundtables.

The FPI's research activities are often carried out in conjunction with SAIS's regional and functional programs dealing with Latin America and the Caribbean Basin, U.S. foreign policy, U.S.-Japan relations, Canada, Africa, Europe, security studies, international energy, and international economics.

FPI publications include the *SAIS Review*, a biannual journal of foreign affairs, which is edited by SAIS students; the SAIS Papers in International Affairs, a monograph series copublished with Westview Press in Boulder, Colorado; and the FPI Policy Briefs, a series of analyses of foreign-policy issues as they develop.

For additional information regarding FPI publications, write to: FPI Publications Program, School of Advanced International Studies, The Johns Hopkins University, 1740 Massachusetts Avenue, N.W., Washington, D.C. 20036.

ABOUT THE BOOK AND AUTHOR

The Soviet Union's gradual but steady accumulation of military power and its consequent evolution as a global strategic actor have affected Western postwar theorems of East-West policy and European security. These paradigms were founded on the assumption that central Europe would remain the primary target for Soviet political-military pressure. Deterring NATO–Warsaw Pact conflict on the central front, therefore, has been the overriding concern of Western security policy. Today, however, Soviet ability to project military power far from its shores has created a new set of geopolitical realities.

Jed Snyder argues that the strategic center of East-West policy may be shifting to "fringe" areas—regions outside central Europe where political-military and economic weakness have created strategic vulnerabilities for the Western Alliance. Although the Soviets will continue to pressure NATO's center (principally West Germany), Moscow can be expected to focus increasing attention on the Mediterranean basin, where the position of the Alliance is deteriorating. Soviet naval and air power have expanded over the entire southern flank at the same time that a discernible erosion of "strategic partnership" has occurred among the five NATO flank states—Turkey, Greece, Italy, Portugal, and Spain. Indigenous sources of sociopolitical instability in the Persian Gulf, the lack of support among gulf states for an effective defense association, and the region's great strategic value for both superpowers suggest that the Persian Gulf may now become a more likely theater of East-West conflict.

The increased strategic importance of these fringe areas creates the need for a Western strategy designed to respond to political-military threats in regions where the comparative investment of the West is dwarfed by that of its adversaries. In this book Jed Snyder examines the sources of Western strategic decline on the southern fringe and calls for a strategy designed to strengthen allied capability to meet a range of security threats.

Jed C. Snyder is deputy director of national security studies and Herman Kahn Fellow at the Hudson Institute. He was senior special assistant to the director of politico-military affairs at the Department of State during the first Reagan administration.

NUMBER 11

SAIS PAPERS IN INTERNATIONAL AFFAIRS

Defending the Fringe

NATO, the Mediterranean, and the Persian Gulf

Jed C. Snyder

The Security Studies Program

WESTVIEW PRESS/BOULDER AND LONDON
WITH THE FOREIGN POLICY INSTITUTE
SCHOOL OF ADVANCED INTERNATIONAL STUDIES
THE JOHNS HOPKINS UNIVERSITY

A Westview Press / Foreign Policy Institute Edition

The drawing on the front cover represents Vauban's "first system"—a city fortification—developed in seventeenth-century France.

This book grew out of the article, "Strategic Bias and Southern Flank Security," by Jed C. Snyder, in *The Washington Quarterly*, © 1985 by The Center for Strategic and International Studies, Georgetown University, and the Massachusetts Institute of Technology.

Published in 1987 in the United States of America by Westview Press, Inc.; Frederick A. Praeger, Publisher; 5500 Central Avenue, Boulder, Colorado 80301

Library of Congress Cataloging-in-Publication Data
Snyder, Jed C.
  Defending the fringe.
  Includes index.
  (SAIS papers in international affairs; no. 11)
  1. North Atlantic Treaty Organization.
2. Mediterranean Region—Defenses. 3. Persian Gulf
Region—Defenses. I. Title. II. Series.
UA646.3.S64 1987   355'.031'091821   86-11182
ISBN 0-8133-0417-2

Composition for this book was created by conversion of the author's word-processor disks. This book was produced without formal editing by the publisher.

∞ The paper used in this publication meets the requirements of the American National Standard for Permanence of Paper for Printed Library Materials Z39.48-1984.

6   5   4   3   2   1

CONTENTS

Part 2
U.S. AND ALLIED SECURITY POLICY IN THE PERSIAN GULF:
OPTIONS AND DILEMMAS

ILLUSTRATIONS

ACRONYMS

AAM	Air-to-air Missile
ACE AMF	Allied Command Europe Mobile Force
AEW	Airborne Early Warning
AFSOUTH	Allied Forces Southern Europe
AIRSOUTH	Allied Air Forces Southern Europe
ASM	Air-to-surface Missile
ASW	Antisubmarine Warfare
AWACS	Airborne Warning and Control System
CENTCOM	U.S. Central Command
CENTO	Central Treaty Organization
CINCEUR	Commander in Chief, United States Forces, Europe
CINCSOUTH	Commander in Chief, Allied Forces Southern Europe
CNO	Chief of Naval Operations
COMAIRSOUTH	Commander, Allied Air Forces Southern Europe
COMNAVSOUTH	Commander, Allied Naval Forces Southern Europe
COMSIXATAF	Commander, Sixth Allied Tactical Air Force
CINCUSNAVEUR	Commander in Chief, U.S. Naval Forces Europe
DECA	Defense and Economic Cooperation Agreement
DEFCON	Defense Condition
DOD	Department of Defense
EEC	European Economic Community
FIR	Flight Information Region
FIVEATAF	Fifth Allied Tactical Air Force
FOB	Forward Operating Base
GCC	Gulf Cooperation Council
GLCM	Ground-launched Cruise Missile
GNP	Gross National Product

IBERLANT	Iberian Atlantic Command
ICBM	Intercontinental Ballistic Missile
IRBM	Intermediate-range Ballistic Missile
INF	Intermediate-range Nuclear Forces
JCS	Joint Chiefs of Staff
LANDSOUTH	Allied Land Forces Southern Europe
LANDSOUTHEAST	Allied Land Forces Southeastern Europe
LANDSOUTHCENT	Allied Land Forces Southern Europe, Central Command
MAB	Marine Amphibious Brigade
MAU	Marine Amphibious Unit
MD	Military District (Soviet Armed Forces)
MPS	Maritime Prepositioning Ships
NADGE	NATO Air-defense Ground Environment
NATO	North Atlantic Treaty Organization
NAVSOUTH	Allied Naval Forces Southern Europe
NTPS	Near-term Prepositioning Ships
OPEC	Organization of Petroleum Exporting Countries
PASOK	Panhellenic Socialist Movement
PLO	Palestine Liberation Organization
RDF	Rapid Deployment Force
RDJTF	Rapid Deployment Joint Task Force
SACEUR	Supreme Allied Commander, Europe
SACLANT	Supreme Allied Commander, Atlantic
SAM	Surface-to-air Missile
SHAPE	Supreme Headquarters, Allied Powers Europe
SIXATAF	Sixth Allied Tactical Air Force
SLOC	Sea Lines of Communication
SNA	Soviet Naval Aviation
SSM	Surface-to-surface Missile
STRIKFORSOUTH	Naval Striking and Support Forces Southern Europe
TVD	Soviet Theater of Operations
UAE	United Arab Emirates
USNAVEUR	U.S. Naval Forces Europe

FOREWORD

This is the second monograph in the series of papers published by Westview Press and The Johns Hopkins Foreign Policy Institute in cooperation with the SAIS Security Studies Program. The first, appropriately, dealt with the impact of Paul Nitze on U.S. postwar strategic thinking. *The Evolution of American Strategic Doctrine: Paul H. Nitze and the Soviet Challenge* was written by Steven L. Rearden, one of the foremost young historians of postwar U.S. national security.

Jed C. Snyder's discussion of the "southern flank" of the NATO theater could not be more timely. Not only is NATO's southern flank increasingly vulnerable, and traditionally ignored, but its geopolitical position abuts the turbulent crescent of the Levant and Persian Gulf. There, critical Western interests must be defended in the absence of a unity of Western action. In a sense, NATO's southern frontiers merge into a gray area in which interests, threats, and allied political divisions are intermingled. Snyder ably addresses these issues.

Our forthcoming study by John H. Maurer, editor of *Orbis*, will examine a historical problem with visible—and controversial—contemporary overtones: *The Short-War Illusions: The Transformation of Military Doctrine During the Opening Campaigns of World War I.*

MICHAEL VLAHOS
Codirector, Security Studies Program
School of Advanced International Studies
Washington, D.C.

ACKNOWLEDGMENTS

The publication of this manuscript culminates the author's tenure as guest scholar at The Johns Hopkins Foreign Policy Institute. I am deeply grateful to Robert E. Osgood and Michael Vlahos for offering me the marvelous opportunity of interacting with the SAIS faculty and students.

Throughout the preparation of this study the SAIS Foreign Policy Institute staff have been extremely patient. In particular, Michael Vlahos has been most understanding and flexible in constantly adjusting the publication timetable to accommodate the author's schedule.

As anyone who has struggled through manuscript preparation knows, the author's responsibility for research and writing often seems to be dwarfed by the infinite number of editorial details that must be attended to in order to produce a professional product. Although the readers will have the final judgment on the substantive content of this monograph, the author can attest to the superb way in which the editorial process was directed by Ms. Nancy McCoy, whose sharp eye focused on the manuscript's weaknesses and whose judgments greatly improved the final product.

A number of colleagues were kind enough to lend their expertise to the project. Their critiques of the manuscript were enormously valuable, and I am most grateful in particular to Lt. General Sinclair Melner, USA (ret.), Mr. Leon Sloss, and Mr. Dean Millot. A number of officials within the U.S. national-security community and at several NATO commands provided critical perspective for many arguments presented here and consented to speak with me anonymously. Finally, I am indebted to Albert and Roberta Wohlstetter, who first encouraged me to investigate the issues discussed in this book and whose intellectual guidance, generosity, and friendship have been so critical to whatever success I enjoy.

Although I have had a great deal of assistance with this book, in the final analysis the author must assume full responsibility for its content.

JED C. SNYDER

INTRODUCTION

Since the formation of the North Atlantic Treaty Organization (NATO) in 1949 Western security concerns have focused principally on central Europe—the area generally agreed to present the greatest potential for East-West conflict. For this reason, most of the Western Alliance's military, political, and economic resources and investment have been directed toward this region. Clearly, one cannot challenge the original logic that dictated such a policy. In the 1950s and 1960s central Europe (primarily the Federal Republic of Germany) was the region most vulnerable to political-military pressure from the Soviet Union. Today, however, there is reason to believe that a number of factors may be converging that could shift the focus of Soviet "interest" away from central Europe toward regions that the West has regarded in the postwar period as theaters of secondary strategic concern. The southern flank of NATO and the Persian Gulf are two candidates.

This potential for a shift in Western security policy stems from changes in the global balance of power and alliance relationships. First and most prominent among these is the Soviet Union's emergence as a global military power and its consequent ability to project its military force far beyond Soviet shores. Second, the Western network of postwar security alliances has contracted so significantly that only Western Europe and the ANZUS Pact allies of the United States—Australia and New Zealand—remain formally linked to the United States by Western multilateral security guarantees. Although the United States maintains a series of critical bilateral agreements with other nations, the image of a seamless web of Western security commitments, fixed firmly in opposition to the Soviet alliance network, has greatly diminished. Third, traditional sources of Western support within NATO are eroding and reducing the nucleus of the Alliance. These factors are encouraging some "fringe" states (for example, those forming NATO's southern periphery) to contemplate seriously alternative forms of political secession, ranging from reassessment of commitments to NATO to consideration of nonaligned or neutral status.

Events of the last decade suggest an evolving shift in the East-West strategic center of gravity, questioning the relevance today of postwar conceptions of Western interests. Western strategic concerns can indeed be endangered by events that occur outside of NATO's formal treaty boundary. Security frameworks defined primarily in geographic terms will come under increasing pressure as "out-of-area" threats to Western security loom larger. If destabilized by internal disruption, regions geographically separated from Europe, such as the the Persian Gulf/ Middle East, might indeed become targets for political and military exploitation by powers (both within and without the region) whose interests do not coincide with those of the West. Such disruption could have a metastatic effect on NATO nations bordering these regions and threaten to embroil the Alliance in a conflict triggered far from NATO's center of gravity. If the conception of Western security interests is broadened, in recognition of postwar changes in the international order and new regions of potential East-West conflict, Eurocentric security frameworks no longer seem sufficient to manage the full range of challenges to those interests.

NATO's Southern Flank

The southern region of NATO presents the Alliance with a range of challenges quite different from—and potentially more critical than— those that NATO faces in other regions within Europe. The deterioration of cooperation among southern flank states and a breakdown in their postwar consensus on Western strategy and defense policy is particularly alarming. Although similar symptoms of Alliance disruption are obvious in other NATO countries, a concentration of stresses in the southern flank threatens to destabilize the region—a region with strategic value that the West is just now beginning to recognize. (This realization was delayed by NATO's tendency to focus its attention on the central front— NATO's historic "central front bias.") A unique concentration of internal political struggles and stresses, including: the Greek-Turkish disputes; Spanish refusal to integrate its military forces into NATO's command structure (codified by the March 12, 1986 public referendum on NATO membership); an unprecedented level of anti-American and anti-Western policy pronouncements from the Papandreou government in Greece; and (with the exception of Turkey) a general leftward shift in the political complexion of governments in southern Europe all have resulted in a rather precarious grouping of allies. The NATO thread linking these nations in a common defensive alliance is beginning to unravel.

Added to these internal stresses is the Soviet threat to the region, most obviously demonstrated by the impressive and expanding Soviet Mediterranean fleet. These two sets of developments seriously challenge the Alliance, and they offer the Warsaw Pact an opportunity to exploit the central region bias of NATO's strategic calculus.

The Persian Gulf

Few regions reflect the divergence of Western and Soviet interests more clearly than the Persian Gulf, where dramatic shifts in the geopolitical balance have raised the value of the region to both superpowers. That divergence is illustrated by a number of trends, including persistent U.S. and Soviet efforts to identify regional surrogates to act as guardians of superpower interests. Moreover, the December 1979 invasion of Afghanistan confirmed that Moscow was willing and able to project its interests into the region, shattering any theories that overt Soviet military initiatives would be permanently limited to the East European sphere of influence. Regional disruption, such as the fall of the shah of Iran, his replacement by a fanatical, fundamentalist regime brought about by cultural-political revolution, as well as the Iran-Iraq War, have highlighted the potential for indigenous conflict and the effect of such conflict on external powers. Furthermore, the continuing civil war in Lebanon testifies to the complex political and religious factionalism that characterizes and energizes much of this volatile region.

The value of the southern flank and the Persian Gulf to Western security interests can be appreciated only when the strategic connection of each region to NATO is understood. This monograph analyzes Western defense concepts and capabilities regarding these two regions. Part 1 assesses the importance of the southern flank of NATO to the Western Alliance. Part 2 discusses Western strategy toward the Persian Gulf and includes a brief historical sketch of U.S. regional security doctrines. In sum, this study calls for the West to broaden its strategic horizon to recognize the evolution of challenges to Western security.

PART 1

NATO AND THE MEDITERRANEAN: SOUTHERN FLANK SECURITY AND THE DECLINE OF STRATEGIC PARTNERSHIP

The Mediterranean Basin

1.
BEYOND THE CENTRAL FRONT

For more than three decades NATO's southern region (which for the purposes of this analysis includes Greece, Turkey, Italy, Spain, and Portugal) has been a subsidiary consideration of Western strategy, which has concentrated its resources and political investment in the central region. The southern flank was treated as a less critical appendage with security interests generally viewed in isolation from central Europe, where the Soviet threat was considered most immediate.

The Strategic Significance of the Southern Region

The security of the center is directly tied to that of the southern flank. The southern flank provides a frontline of defense. For example, as one of only two NATO states bordering the Soviet Union, Turkey—depending on the axis of Soviet attack—could act to shield the center from Soviet pressure. In addition, any campaign by the Soviets to destabilize central Europe is likely to be initiated on the flank, where NATO is politically and militarily less prepared for conflict and is also politically more vulnerable.

Currently, NATO conventional forces are vastly outnumbered by the Warsaw Pact forces in the center and on the flank. Additionally, in a southern flank contingency NATO forces would initially be limited to Greek and Turkish troops rather than an integrated NATO force—that is, one including military units from a number of NATO countries. The United States—alone or in concert with its NATO allies—could bring considerable air, sea, and land assets to bear, but since the decision to commit such forces would be a function of political will as much as the availability of resources and logistical management, it is questionable

3

whether they can be depended upon to arrive early enough in a conflict to affect the military outcome.

Finally, the Soviets' potential for "lightning strikes" and surprise on the southern flank may enable them to engage NATO forces in a limited campaign, thereby avoiding escalation and a wider theater of conflict that would include central Europe. This potential results, in part, from the character of strategic warning. Soviet preparations for an attack could assume a variety of models, depending on a number of military factors, including mobilization requirements, disposition of forces, alert rates, etc. If the preparations for an attack are gradual, the warning may appear ambiguous to NATO military authorities, delaying a Western decision on how or whether to respond. Moreover, NATO's evaluation of warning would occur within a political as well as a military context. The more ambiguous the warning, the greater potential for delay in coming to a decision that could place great political strains on European allies.

Although there is no postwar precedent for a direct Soviet military attack on Western Europe, the failure of the Western allies to anticipate a Soviet invasion of Afghanistan, despite intelligence gathered over several months indicating that an attack was imminent, does cast a shadow over the Alliance's will as well as its ability to recognize and act on warning of imminent aggression. Clearly, Afghanistan was viewed as "out-of-area," whereas presumably a Soviet transgression against a NATO member would be treated as a more serious incursion. Nevertheless, it is possible that ambiguous warning may provide an excuse for NATO to delay responding until a situation is clarified, as happened prior to the 1979 Soviet invasion of Afghanistan. (A threat to Turkey, however, would supposedly trigger a more timely Western response.) Even if signals of Soviet troop movements against a NATO state or preparations for such deployments are absolutely clear, they may be received with insufficient warning to allow the NATO crisis alert system to function as it is designed. In addition, the large numbers of Warsaw Pact forces stationed on the borders of Greece and Turkey increase the potential for a "standing start" attack.

There are indications that Soviet strategic goals in central Europe and the current state of allied vulnerability on the southern flank may reinforce each other. Soviet planners are fully aware of the logistical and political difficulties with which NATO would be faced in the event of a crisis in the southern region. NATO military leaders would be reluctant to reinforce the flank in a crisis if that reinforcement came at the expense of the center, for any threat of conflict on the flank would probably be seen as a serious threat to the center as well. Obviously, this calculation would depend heavily on the context of the crisis.

Moreover, any response of the Supreme Allied Commander, Europe (SACEUR) and of NATO ministers would be affected by their calculation of the current political climate in Europe. It would also be affected by whether the central front allies viewed a Soviet attack on the flank as a first step toward a European-wide war and therefore concluded that a decision to reinforce the southern region would be dangerous and premature, as it might leave central Europe exposed.

In sum, Soviet strategy in Europe could be shifting toward the exploitation of both the Western tendency to focus on central Europe and NATO's reluctance to address seriously the deteriorating political and military position in the south, in order to realize a long-held strategic goal—creating wedges between the allies by pressuring the Alliance where it is least likely to resist that pressure successfully. In that sense, Soviet strategy simply reinforces NATO's weaknesses.

The allies have been unwilling to face a politically painful paradox. Effective deterrence of conflict requires adequate defensive preparations. An investment in such a defense would reduce the likelihood that a crisis involving the flank and possibly all of Europe would ever materialize. NATO, however, has been so myopic about central Europe that any program to strengthen the south has often been regarded as antithetical to NATO's major concern—the defense of West Germany—even though a strengthening of the flank might reasonably be calculated to force the Soviets to alter their estimates concerning *any* campaign in Europe.

Finally, NATO's only rapid reinforcement capability—the Allied Command Europe (ACE) Mobile Force (AMF)—is only a "paper" force, drawing units from the central front as well as from other areas. The AMF is not "in place." Although it was developed primarily for flank defense, its rapid deployment capability is in question, in part because its exercises have been infrequent.

Several of NATO's political and military leaders have called attention to the Alliance's historical tendency to diminish the southern flank's critical role in NATO's larger strategy and to the propensity to underplay the unique internal stresses in the region that undermine NATO's ability to grapple with the increasingly worrisome Soviet military challenges in the Mediterranean. In 1975 General T. R. Milton, former U.S. representative to NATO's Military Committee, wrote that a stable flank was vital to the Alliance's task of defending Europe as a whole and that the combination of internal stresses and poor state of readiness presented a "pretty shaky consortium, held together—to the extent that it is together—by the United States commitment to the Mediterranean."[1] In 1978 British Admiral Sir Peter Hill Norton, former chairman of NATO's Military Committee, concluded that the military situation on the flank was reparable, but only if the peculiar economic and political stresses in the region were resolved.[2]

NATO security analysts have also begun to examine the vulnerabilities of the southern flank. An Atlantic Council study published in 1981 concluded that the combination of growing Soviet naval strength in the Mediterranean, potential bases in Libya, Syria, and Iraq, and increasing numbers of Soviet long-range air assets committed to the southern tier all worsen the prospects for flank security. The study noted with alarm that during this period the United States had been forced to redeploy to the Indian Ocean 1 of the 2 aircraft carriers previously stationed permanently in the Mediterranean.[3] The extent of the NATO–Warsaw Pact force asymmetry in the southern region is clearly described in NATO's 1984 force comparison study, which estimates that the total NATO ground strength available in a southern flank contingency would be 45 divisions against 64 Warsaw Pact divisions.[4] The air balance is even more asymmetrical.

Clearly, there are limits to the amount of force the Soviets would be willing to utilize in the south, depending on Soviet intentions and intelligence estimates of NATO strength in the region. They would also be concerned about draining forces from central Europe in the event of a flank crisis. In sum, in contemplating an attack on NATO's southern flank, Soviet planners would face some of the same constraints and obstacles that NATO would confront. Ultimately, however, the superior strength of Soviet military forces in the region and the current state of political disharmony among the NATO flank states would combine to reduce the perceived risk of a Soviet military operation in the Mediterranean basin.

Traditionally, the "southern flank" has been thought to consist of the five member states along the southern tier of Europe, an unbroken phalanx stretching from the Azores to Turkey. This of course is a misconception; it disregards geographical discontinuities and the interspersion of non-NATO states along the northern Mediterranean coast. In addition, because the NATO states of the region have for the most part been considered capable of only limited defense of their own territories against Soviet aggression, the responsibility for overall defense of the area has rested almost entirely on the U.S. strategic deterrent and the U.S. Sixth Fleet. In short, the notion of a southern flank consisting only of NATO members is accurate within the narrow context of the NATO Alliance. But the strategic concept must embrace the Mediterranean basin as a whole, and NATO should expand the framework through which it assesses potential Western assets in the region. Non-NATO members in the region whose location will be strategic in the event of conflict and whose policies might, during a crisis, become pro-Western—Yugoslavia, for example—should be included in contingency planning.

Additionally, much of the full range of U.S. strategic interests in the region is obscured when discussion of "Middle Eastern" problems is limited to what have always been considered the three prominent U.S. policy concerns there: the security of Israel, a maintained flow of oil to the West, and support for such moderate/conservative Arab states and Gulf sheikhdoms as Saudi Arabia, Egypt, Jordan, Morocco, and Oman. Developments over the past five years have shown that indigenous political conflicts in the Persian Gulf/Middle East region are the most immediate threat to political stability, with Soviet exploitation of those conflicts perhaps rating as the second most pressing dilemma for Western policy.

As the Mediterranean links the southern flank to the Middle East, any conflict in the gulf region could easily spill over into areas within NATO's formal treaty boundaries, although recent regional conflicts, notably those between Iran and Iraq and in Lebanon have been contained. Two instances that would run a high risk of spillover are (a) a Soviet threat to Western oil resources, or (b) a prolongation of any future Arab-Israeli conflict resulting in violations of NATO airspace by the Soviets in order to deliver supplies to their clients. In sum, the stability of the flank may directly affect the security of much of the gulf region and vice versa.

The Mediterranean assumes great importance for the Alliance for the following reasons:

- Its role as the most intensely utilized maritime corridor of the world, important to both Europe and the USSR, and especially its function as a sea line of communication (SLOC) to Persian Gulf and North African oil resources for European allies. Over 50 percent of the petroleum imported by Europe arrives via the Mediterranean. Although land pipelines could reduce dependency on the Mediterranean, the reduction would not be sufficient to alter significantly the situation. The Soviet Union receives over 50 percent of its imports and ships 60 percent of it exports through the Mediterranean. The Soviet Union's ability to reduce significantly its dependence on the Mediterranean as a SLOC is geographically more restricted than the West's;
- Its role as the only Soviet naval and maritime egress from the Black Sea to the Indian and Atlantic oceans; and,
- Its potential for NATO and independent U.S. military operations and base areas; for Western power projection to the Persian Gulf/

Middle East, and North Africa; and as a strategic rear area for NATO's central front states.

Soviet Interests and Vulnerabilities on the Flank

The southern region is and will continue to be a key factor in the broader context of U.S. global strategy to restrict Soviet expansion to the south; the Mediterranean will remain an area of major concern for the Soviets. Their greatest vulnerability is from the south, where the principal Soviet industrial regions are potentially vulnerable to attack from theater air forces and where critical lines of communication supporting Soviet forces in Eastern Europe are vulnerable. Paradoxically, it also represents an area where NATO and the United States lack significant military capability to exploit Soviet weaknesses. The Mediterranean presents both the Warsaw Pact and the Western Alliance with a number of security quandries that could be regarded as threats and/or opportunities for both, including the following:

The Black Sea Exits. Control of the Black Sea exits would allow the Soviets to reinforce their Mediterranean squadron with sufficient strength to challenge the U.S. Sixth Fleet. The Turkish straits would become one of several key Soviet objectives on the southern flank if war in that region seemed imminent. Soviet naval reinforcement planning would depend principally on the contingency. The Soviets could reinforce their Mediterranean fleet before any sea war began. If the Soviet Union sought to deal a crippling initial blow to the U.S. fleet, control of the Black Sea would be less critical. If, however, a long sea campaign was envisioned, then reinforcement would be a greater priority for both sides.

Control of Oil. Soviet control or denial of Persian Gulf oil to the NATO Alliance could be catastrophic. Denial of petroleum resources or control of both access and price could seriously injure the economies of Western Europe and Japan. These states depend on the gulf for a significant percent of their energy supplies. Despite a decline in the worldwide demand for oil, West European dependence on Persian Gulf oil will not be significantly reduced for the foreseeable future.[5] As former U.S. secretary of defense Harold Brown has written, the European allies and Japan "do not have the choice of managing without Persian Gulf oil."[6] Should the Soviets seek to increase their pressure (either by threatening to seize the oil fields or by more subtle political arguments) on key OPEC (Organization of Petroleum Exporting Countries) suppliers, a strengthened allied naval presence in the Mediterranean (including U.S. and allied ships) might offset that pressure. Considering the size of the Soviet Mediterranean fleet, allied naval reinforcement would have to be significant to have any appreciable effect on Soviet behavior. As the size of the U.S. and Soviet fleets grew in such a crisis, so would the risk of superpower confrontation.

Interdiction of the Lines of Communication. NATO's naval lines of communication are critically important. In time of war, the majority of war matériel to the peninsular nations of Italy, Greece, and Turkey would come by sea.

Fracturing of the Alliance. A Soviet military initiative on the southern flank may encourage the secession of Turkey and Greece from NATO. As the noted French strategist Pierre Hassner has observed, these countries have already been at times in a state of "semi-withdrawal."[7] Soviet military pressure on the flank could also remove any hope that future Spanish governments could be compelled to integrate Spanish forces into NATO's command structure.

It is not clear that an actual Soviet seizure of territory would be required to cause key states to withdraw from, or alter their military contribution to, the Alliance. Political pressure (similar to that applied by Moscow against Turkey when Ankara decided to accept U.S. Jupiter intermediate-range ballistic missiles [IRBMs] in the late 1950s) might be sufficient to elicit pledges of neutrality or nonbelligerence.

Potential for a Fait Accompli. The southern region constitutes one of the few areas in NATO where the Soviet Union might execute a lightning strike and seize a small amount of territory before NATO was able to respond effectively. The assumption that an attack on the flank would come *only* as the result of an all-out attack on Europe is no longer credible, due in part to the peculiar vulnerabilities of the flank and the considerable Soviet military presence in the Mediterranean and on the Turkish border. As mentioned earlier, Moscow might see such an attack not only as a lesser risk than a general military campaign in Europe, but also as a highly probable means of precipitating an Alliance-wide crisis that would lead to NATO's political disintegration. Thus, the Soviets could achieve their goal of splitting NATO without a major NATO–Warsaw Pact war.

The combination of questionable reinforcement capability and the lack of a NATO integrated force on the Turkish border would complicate the political-military decisionmaking process should a crisis occur in the Mediterranean region. If NATO failed to respond militarily to a Soviet incursion, the United States would be faced with a critical policy decision, since U.S. forces could be lifted to the region fairly quickly. This would, however, be a unilateral decision by Washington. The character of a U.S.-NATO response to such an incursion would be a key factor in further Soviet actions. A unilateral U.S. deployment would indicate refusal by the NATO council to participate in a military response, since it is very doubtful that the United States would *prefer* to act unilaterally. Soviet planners could deduce from this that military initiatives elsewhere in Europe (perhaps on the northern flank) would meet with the same lack of allied response, with the United States unable or unwilling to respond unilaterally because of other commitments.

Regardless, the Soviet leadership would certainly weigh all such factors in determining how far it was willing to proceed in testing Alliance solidarity in a crisis. For this and other reasons, U.S. and NATO contingency planning for political-military crises in the southern region should be developed in harmony. The range of plausible Soviet military campaigns on the southern flank should be reviewed periodically as Soviet forces in the region are modernized and/or shifted. More important, greater effort must be made to coordinate U.S. war plans for the region with NATO contingency planning in advance of a conflict so that the long (and potentially disastrous) delays produced by political and military consultation within the NATO council will be held to a minimum.

2.
AFSOUTH COMMAND STRUCTURE

The southern region is by far the largest of the four areas in Allied Command Europe (ACE), stretching four thousand kilometers from the Strait of Gibraltar to the eastern border of Turkey and about fourteen hundred kilometers from the North African littoral to the Alps. The southern flank command area covers 1.5 million square miles. Allied Forces Southern Europe (AFSOUTH) was established in June 1951 and has survived a number of disruptive command changes. These have included the French government's decision to withdraw from NATO's Integrated Military Structure in 1966. France was one of six allies— along with Greece, Italy, the United Kingdom, the United States, and Italy—*originally* contributing forces to AFSOUTH. In addition, the decision by Greece to withdraw from NATO in 1974 in protest over the Turkish invasion of Cyprus further weakened the command structure. Greece's return to the Alliance's military wing in 1980 was only partial, since a number of key command and control issues have remained unresolved, operationally limiting Greece's military contribution.

NATO members currently contributing forces to AFSOUTH are the United States, the United Kingdom, Turkey, Greece, Italy, and Portugal.[8] (French naval forces remain in the Mediterranean and participate in exercises—a potentially important factor in a crisis.) The *Commander in Chief, Allied Forces Southern Europe* (CINCSOUTH) is one of three major commanders reporting to SACEUR. The five principal commands of AFSOUTH are as follows.

- *Allied Land Forces Southern Europe* (LANDSOUTH), commanded by an Italian four-star general with headquarters in Verona, Italy, is responsible for NATO defense of Northeast Italy.

TABLE 1
Allied Forces Southern Europe

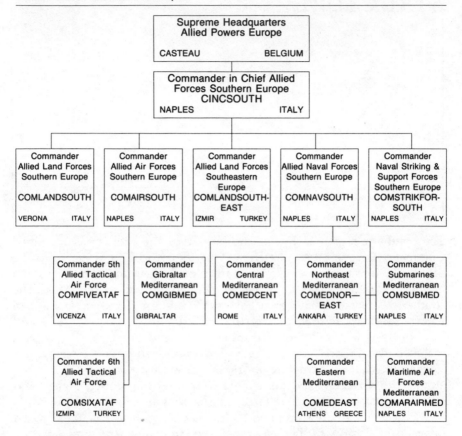

- *Allied Land Forces Southeastern Europe* (LANDSOUTHEAST), commanded by a Turkish four-star general with headquarters in Izmir, Turkey, is responsible for the NATO defense of Turkey.
- *Allied Naval Forces Southern Europe* (NAVSOUTH), commanded by an Italian four-star admiral with headquarters in Naples, Italy, is responsible for the defense of the SLOC from Gibraltar to the Black Sea, as well as naval maritime air operations. Although no ships are permanently assigned to the NAVSOUTH commander in peacetime, a multinational naval task force is activated twice a year for month-long exercises.[9] In wartime COMNAVSOUTH assumes control of seven subordinate naval commands. Although the U.S. Sixth Fleet is the major allied naval force in the Mediterranean, French, Italian, Greek, Turkish, Portuguese, and Spanish vessels should be included in any net assessment of allied naval power in the

region. The French, Italian, and Spanish contingents—each of which includes aircraft carriers—are particularly important.

- *Naval Striking and Support Forces Southern Europe* (STRIKFORSOUTH) is the NATO designation for the U.S. Sixth Fleet, commanded by a U.S. vice admiral, with home port in Gaeta, Italy. This command has essentially two missions: to establish sea control of the Mediterranean and to "influence" the outcome of the land battle ashore.
- *Allied Air Forces Southern Europe* (AIRSOUTH), commanded by a U.S. Air Force lieutenant general with headquarters in Naples, Italy, is responsible for all land-based air operations throughout the AFSOUTH region. There are two commands under the commander, COMAIRSOUTH: the Fifth Allied Tactical Air Force (FIVEATAF) based in Vicenza, Italy, and the Sixth Allied Tactical Air Force (SIXATAF) in Izmir, Turkey. In peacetime AIRSOUTH's primary role is to maintain air-defense capabilities.

Discussions continue between AFSOUTH and the Greek general staff to establish a sixth command, a NATO land and air headquarters at Larissa in Greece—LANDSOUTHCENT—including a newly designated air command—the Seventh Allied Tactical Air Force (SEVENATAF). A simmering dispute between Greece and Turkey over military jurisdiction in the Aegean Sea has delayed establishment of this new command.[10]

The geography of the southern region places severe constraints on the NATO commanders in the region. One can divide the flank into five separate theaters of operation: Thrace (northern Greece/western Turkey), northern Italy, eastern Turkey, the Mediterranean Sea, and the Iberian Peninsula. The geographical constraints in the AFSOUTH region present its three land commanders with unique problems of planning and strategy. They are separated from each other by about a thousand kilometers, which greatly complicates attempts to develop an integrative approach to regional defense. The Mediterranean links the three principal land theaters together and is thus critical to the defense of the AFSOUTH region. As former CINCSOUTH (and current chairman of the Joint Chiefs of Staff) Admiral William J. Crowe, Jr., has noted, the land commanders cannot plan for mutual support nor can CINCSOUTH shift forces from one AFSOUTH theater to another over land.[11] While airlift will be available, transfers of troops and material will be heavily dependent upon sealift.

3.
THE MEDITERRANEAN THEATER: THE GEOSTRATEGIC LINK

The Mediterranean theater, although historically an area of great strategic importance, has not received sufficient attention by either NATO or the United States until recently. The Mediterranean's strategic renaissance has been prompted by several factors, including a dramatic increase over the last fifteen years in Soviet naval deployments and capabilities in the region, paralleling a 1979 U.S. Navy decision to reduce temporarily the U.S. carrier presence in the Mediterranean from 2 to about 1-1/3.* As a result of an increased threat from Libya and the 1986 Gulf of Sidra crisis, the navy has decided to return to the previous two-carrier commitment.[12]

The Mediterranean washes the shores of eighteen nations with a total population approaching 300 million people. Politically, as well as socially and ethnically, it contains a diverse, heterogenous collection of alliances. The southern littoral of the sea consists of non-NATO countries with varying degrees of military capability and political alignment to the East and the West. Nations of the northern littoral, with the exception of Albania and Yugoslavia, are members of NATO.

Although the Mediterranean is not a large body of water, it touches three continents—Europe, Africa, and Asia. Its length between the Strait of Gibraltar and the Gulf of Iskenderun in Turkey is 2,100 miles; its maximum width—between El Agheila and Trieste—is 600 miles. The two large basins—east and west—are separated by the peninsular nation

---

*A 1-1/3 carrier presence means, operationally, 1 carrier on station twelve months a year and 2 carriers, four months a year.

of Italy. The eastern basin includes two semi-enclosed seas, the Adriatic and the Aegean.

Control of the Mediterranean Sea requires dominance over the various narrow straits and adjacent coastal areas. At present the straits are bordered by NATO or friendly countries with the exception of the Strait of Otranto. Control of this strait can be challenged by Albania or Yugoslavia. In the western Mediterranean the 8-1/2-mile wide Strait of Gibraltar controls the Atlantic passage. The two basins are connected by the 90-mile wide Strait of Sicily, separating Italy from the African nation of Tunisia. It is principally through this passage that naval support could reach Italy and NATO's southeastern powers—Greece and Turkey. The Suez Canal provides another transit route, should Egypt decide to lend its support. In sum, the support of non-NATO states on the southern littoral would be critical to allied resupply operations.

In the east the waterways joining the Mediterranean and the Black Sea lie within Turkish territory. Turkish control over the Bosporus and the Dardanelles denies the Soviets full realization of Russia's historical aspirations in the Middle East. Turkish control of the straits could restrict the movement of the Soviet Black Sea Fleet, although the current state of the Turkish navy would make such an operation difficult. These straits form the passage to the Black Sea, with the many islands in the Aegean dominating the Mediterranean approaches to the straits.

Egyptian control of naval traffic through the Suez Canal would be the key to any Western naval reinforcement from the Middle East. Here, Egypt's policy toward the Soviet Union could be a major factor. Egyptian President Hosni Mubarak's recent reopening of diplomatic relations with Moscow creates the possibility that the Egyptian government might oppose any Israeli efforts to assist NATO in a Mediterranean contingency and that Israel might risk retaliation from the Soviet Union.

The U.S. Naval Presence

For most of its life the U.S. Mediterranean fleet (the Sixth Fleet) was composed of 2 aircraft carriers and an embarked U.S. Marine force, a total of 35 to 40 ships, including escorts and replenishment vessels. Each of the 2 carriers supported roughly 85 combat aircraft of current vintage. From 4 to 7 amphibious ships lifted a battalion landing team and its support, roughly 2,000 marines. Viewed as part of the overall U.S. contribution to NATO, the resources of the Sixth Fleet are not trivial. Table 2 shows the 2-carrier composition of the U.S. Sixth Fleet.

The Sixth Fleet's surface forces routinely operated as three distinct groups: 2 carrier task groups and an amphibious task group. Each group was assigned a portion of the cruiser/destroyer escorts. While operations

TABLE 2
The U.S. Mediterranean Fleet (1985–1986)

---

2 aircraft carriers
14 surface combatants/escorts (cruisers/destroyers)
5 amphibious ships (lift for a marine amphibious unit)
12 auxiliary ships
1 P–3 Orion antisubmarine warfare squadron
4 attack submarines

Source: Data from Norman Polmar, *The Ships and Aircraft of the U.S. Fleet*, 13th ed. (Annapolis, Md.: Naval Institute Press, 1984), 14.

sometimes covered the entire Mediterranean, the carriers developed a pattern that usually had 1 carrier task group in the central Mediterranean's Ionian Sea and another in the western Mediterranean.[13]

By design and deployment the fleet has primarily been a projection force, as distinct from a sea control force. In this connection its importance to Western Europe's defense has always been its availability forward, where deployed aircraft and marines could participate early in any theater land engagement. From the early 1950s, however, when the fleet first acquired a nuclear-strike capability, until the mid-1960s, when secretary of defense Robert McNamara relieved the carriers of their strategic alert retaliatory mission, projection warfare primarily meant nuclear strikes.[14] The emphasis subsequently has been on conventional power projection, although a substantial nuclear capability remains.

The Sixth Fleet's ability to project power has not been consistent, however, due to fluctuations in deployment patterns. From 1979 until March 1986 only 1 carrier operated continuously in the Mediterranean, and in that configuration it was unlikely that the Sixth Fleet would play a major role in a conventional battle, since concern over the vulnerability of a lone carrier to Soviet bombers would dictate early removal in the event of conflict. Virtually 65 percent of the roughly 85 carrier-based combat aircraft must be reserved for the defensive mission in wartime. That leaves relatively few aircraft to carry out offensive missions. The author's recent conversations with U.S. naval planners suggest that in its 1-carrier configuration a decision would have already been made to protect the lone Sixth Fleet carrier by "preemptively" withdrawing it from the eastern Mediterranean: "The CNO [Chief of Naval Operations] would never allow *one* carrier to steam east of Sicily in the event of a conflict; two maybe."

Periodically, proposals have been made to change Sixth Fleet deployments. For example, former secretary of defense James Schlesinger discussed the possibility of ending continuous deployments in favor of a flexible deployment scheme that would rotate other ships in and out of the Mediterranean and surge ships into the region during a crisis.[15] It is unlikely, however, that a surge of U.S. carriers into the Mediterranean in the event of a crisis would be approved by the Joint Chiefs of Staff (JCS) unless the carriers were reinforced heavily, a transfer of naval power that would draw down the strength of other fleets. In addition, it is unclear whether the surge could be deployed in a timely fashion. In such a situation allied naval assets could be a critical variable.

Efforts to bolster U.S. naval forces in the Persian Gulf/Indian Ocean in the wake of the Iranian revolution and the December 1979 Soviet invasion of Afghanistan have come at the expense of the Sixth and Seventh fleets. From 1951 until the Iranian revolution and the subsequent taking of U.S. hostages, 2 carrier task forces were deployed continuously in the Mediterranean.[16] The Sixth Fleet has been a potent and flexible instrument of U.S. power in the Mediterranean, playing a major role in a variety of crises from Greece in 1947 through the 1973 Arab-Israeli War, the 1982–84 U.S. Marine deployment in Lebanon, and the Gulf of Sidra crises in 1981 and 1986.

This discussion suggests the importance of the southern region as a vital link between two areas of key U.S. concern—Europe and the Persian Gulf/Middle East. More directly, it implies the need for a strategy that links the Persian Gulf and the Mediterranean, particularly regarding the deployment of naval assets. Naval exercises involving both the Indian Ocean and the Mediterranean fleets would enable planning staffs to visualize the operational link between these two theaters. In addition, recent changes in peacetime command responsibilities should allow greater flexibility in exercising naval forces in the region. CINCSOUTH, for example, now has parallel command of U.S. Naval Forces Europe (USNAVEUR). Previously, CINCSOUTH assumed the post of commander in chief, U.S. Naval Forces Europe (CINCUSNAVEUR) only in wartime. Giving CINCSOUTH a U.S. "hat" should improve peacetime (including crisis) command and control. The March–April 1986 Libyan crisis, for example, was managed more efficiently than previous naval operations in part because the theater commander (CINCSOUTH) had the ability to move naval forces quickly as a *U.S.* commander.

Fleet Operations

The Sixth Fleet has a fairly secure logistical peacetime network in the Mediterranean, maintaining access to NATO bases in Greece, Turkey, and Spain. This is true, however, only in the NATO context. If the Sixth Fleet was to assume a *unilateral* role, for example, in support of Israel during another Arab-Israeli conflict, its access would be questionable, as key NATO allies might be reluctant to assist the United States in a non-NATO operation. Recall, for example, the refusal of Turkey to assist the United States in its efforts to resupply Israel in the 1973 Arab-Israeli War.

The availability of Greek bases to support the Sixth Fleet will become doubtful should Prime Minister Andreas Papandreou implement his public threats to close all U.S. bases in Greece by 1988. The most critical U.S. base is the Souda Bay complex on the northwest side of Crete near Canea (Khaniá). Souda Bay is the Sixth Fleet's most important anchorage in the eastern Mediterranean. It is a naturally protected anchorage, large enough for nearly the entire fleet. In addition, it acts as a storage depot for petroleum, oil, and lubricants, and ammunition for NATO forces. Adjacent to the port is an airfield capable of supporting C–141 transport aircraft. Loss of Souda Bay would deprive the Sixth Fleet of a key anchorage that may be irreplaceable in the near term.

The continued operation of U.S. bases in the southern region can no longer be taken for granted. Only after protracted negotiations in 1982 between the governments of Greece and the United States was agreement finally reached on the continued U.S. use of bases (including naval access to Souda Bay). The negotiations were drawn out because of demonstrations protesting the U.S. presence (intensified as a result of the October 1981 election of the socialist Papandreou government) and Greek insistence on a larger annual military aid package from the United States.

The use of U.S. aid as a bargaining tool in the base rights talks has become a larger problem with other southern flank states as well, including Spain and Portugal. The Sixth Fleet can operate (and indeed has operated) without an extensive basing network; but the availability of allied bases has enabled the U.S. Navy to sustain its presence at the lowest possible cost in fleet assets. Its ability to "show the flag" has proven significant in a number of instances, including the 1981 and 1986 Gulf of Sidra incidents (in which several Libyan combat aircraft were shot down by U.S. carrier-based planes) and U.S. naval support for Israel during the 1967 and 1973 Arab-Israeli wars. The Sixth Fleet also serves as a constant reminder to Syria that a Soviet presence in that country will not be unopposed by the United States.

The Soviet Naval Challenge

The Soviet Mediterranean fleet, the Fifth Escadra, began its deployment in 1964 as a small component of the Soviet Black Sea Fleet. Prior to this the only Soviet naval presence in the region consisted of

4 W-class submarines based in Albania at Vlorë, where the Soviets had established a base in 1958. In 1961 Albania sided with the People's Republic of China in the first public evidence of a Sino-Soviet dispute, resulting in the Soviet loss of that naval installation.

By the end of the 1960s the Soviet Union emerged as a substantial naval power. Its Mediterranean fleet was seen by a number of Arab states as potentially supportive in an Arab-Israeli conflict. Increasingly close Soviet political ties with Syria, Libya, and Egypt ensured the availability of friendly ports to the Soviets while at the same time making increasingly unwelcome any Western military presence. The Soviet fleet's strength became a lever of influence in the region that in the late 1960s and early 1970s began to rival that of the Sixth Fleet. Early deployments in the Mediterranean were the first Soviet attempts to create a self-sustaining naval force far from friendly ports. Initial operations were modest and generally limited to anchorages in international waters, mostly off Tunisia. Although the Soviet Mediterranean force of the early 1960s was more a nuisance to the West than a threat, the occasional sighting of Soviet intelligence vessels did cause alterations in U.S. naval strategy in the region. These early Soviet deployments differed substantially from those of the West. In particular, the Soviets had no aircraft carriers, but they had a large submarine force. That submarine force has expanded and the Soviets have begun to deploy carriers as well. The year 1979 marked two signal events—the maiden voyage of the carrier *Minsk* in the Mediterranean, and the first Soviet dual-carrier task-group operation involving the *Minsk* and the *Kiev*. The Soviet navy now includes 3 Kiev-class carriers (with an additional one on sea trials), and 2 Moskva-class ASW helicopter carriers; a 70,000 ton nuclear-powered carrier is under construction.[17] All 7 carriers have been built at the Nikolayev shipyard on the Black Sea.

The Montreux Convention

The Montreux Convention, signed in 1936, governs both peacetime and wartime transit through the Mediterranean. It defines naval access rights to the straits of the Bosporus and the Dardanelles. The document is complex, but the salient points can be briefly described:

- Complete freedom of transit for merchant vessels of all nations (in peace and war) provided Turkey is not a belligerent.
- Restriction of warships of non–Black Sea powers in their passage to, and length of stay in, the Black Sea. The maximum aggregate tonnage for *all* non–Black Sea powers within the Black Sea at any one time may not exceed 30,000 tons or in certain exceptional

circumstances, 45,000 tons. This is a crucial clause, as it effectively prohibits all modern surface combatants and carriers of non–Black Sea states from transit. *No restriction is placed on capital ships of Black Sea powers provided they pass through the straits singly.*
- Restriction of the passage of submarines, including a provision permitting Black Sea powers to bring submarines purchased from outside powers into the Black Sea for repair only and permitting them to leave.
- No guns larger than 8 inches (203 mm) to be carried by ships of non–Black Sea powers.
- Curtailment of passage of warships of nonbelligerent powers in time of war except in extraordinary humanitarian circumstances. *If Turkey is a belligerent party, or believes itself to be in imminent danger of war, the Turkish government has the right to close the straits to the passage of warships of any and all nations.*
- At least eight days notice to be provided to the Turkish government through diplomatic channels of the transit of any warships through the straits.[18]

This convention, which obviously favors Black Sea navies (including the Soviet Union's), does place some significant restrictions on the deployment of combatants. To this day, for example, Soviet submarines may transit the straits during daytime only and on the surface only. During any conflict the Turkish straits (the Bosporus, the Sea of Marmara, and the Dardanelles) could legally be closed by the Turks, prohibiting reinforcement of the Fifth Escadra from the Black Sea. Together with the closure of the other two entrances to the Mediterranean—Gibraltar and the Suez Canal—this would effectively seal off the entire region from Soviet naval reinforcement. For this reason the Soviet Union has significantly increased its Mediterranean fleet to reduce the need for reinforcement from its other three fleets—the Northern, Pacific, and Baltic.

The Soviet peacetime naval mission does not differ significantly from that of the United States—power projection to a region where the maintenance of its interests requires constant naval surveillance and support for regional allies. However, the straits are important to the Soviets not only as a military route but also as a commercial one. After Turkey, the Soviet Union is the largest user of the straits, with 62 percent of its naval trade passing through them.[19]

The Black Sea Fleet provides surface warships and aircraft for operations in the Mediterranean through the Fifth Escadra. Submarine deployments to the Mediterranean are provided from the Northern Fleet.

TABLE 3
The Soviet Mediterranean Squadron (Fifth Escadra) (1985–1986)

6–8 torpedo attack submarines
1 or 2 cruise missile attack submarines
1 or 2 missile cruisers
6–8 destroyers and frigates
1–3 minesweepers
1–3 amphibious ships
15–20 auxiliary ships
5 or 6 survey, research, and intelligence collection-ships

Source: Data from Norman Polmar, Guide to the Soviet Navy, 3d ed. (Annapolis, Md.: Naval Institute Press, 1983), 19.

A typical "snapshot" of the Fifth Escadra deployments is shown in Table 3.

The Soviet naval assets in the Black Sea and Mediterranean comprise a formidable force. In addition to support from land-based aircraft based in the Crimea, helicopter carriers of the Moskva class are based in the Black Sea and operate regularly in the Mediterranean as do the Kiev-class carriers when they are deployed in the theater. Several statistics on Black Sea deployments highlight the strategic value the Soviet Union places on the fleet and the southern theater. First, the Black Sea Fleet has the largest cruiser-destroyer force in any of the Soviet fleets. Second, the fleet has 27 percent of the navy's major combatants. Finally, including the Caspian Sea Flotilla, the Black Sea Fleet has 25 percent of the Soviet navy's aircraft.[20]

The issue of sustainability is central to the naval balance of power in the Mediterranean. The Soviets have learned this lesson as a result of their expulsion from Egypt by president Anwar Sadat, losing use of all Egyptian air bases in 1972 and all naval facilities in 1976.[21] That event provoked the construction of underway replenishment ships that allow the Soviets a greater open-ocean presence, which would be valuable in a crisis.

Soviet access to Egyptian ports began during the 1967 Arab-Israeli War when, after the Egyptian sinking of the Israeli destroyer Eilat, Soviet ships moved into Port Said and Alexandria, ostensibly to place themselves between Israeli and Egyptian vessels to prevent Israeli retaliation for the sinking. Egyptian president Gamal Abdel Nasser welcomed the Soviet presence which lasted until the Sadat expulsion. The loss of Egyptian bases may not be permanent, however. Meanwhile, the Soviets may be able to gain access to Libyan bases (Tripoli or Benghazi) in an emergency.

The loss of naval access to Alexandria has had a significant effect on Soviet submarine deployments. Prior to that access Soviet submarines were in almost constant rotation from their home fleets in the Baltic and North seas, with fairly short deployments in the Mediterranean. The ability to anchor at Alexandria allowed much longer tours in the region. It is worth noting the recent Israeli reports of construction at the Syrian port of Tartus of a Soviet submarine tender, which if expanded, would give the Soviets an anchorage in the extreme eastern Mediterranean.[22] The Soviet submarine threat to the Sixth Fleet and allied navies is acute; in a crisis preceded by weeks of escalation and reinforcement, the total Soviet Mediterranean submarine force could exceed 35 in number.[23] This would argue for an increased U.S.-NATO ASW effort, although such operations are difficult in the Mediterranean due to particular characteristics, including temperature fluctuations and geographic barriers. Increasing the submarine component of the Sixth Fleet should be considered, in light of an emerging Soviet threat to U.S. surface ships.

The threat posed by Soviet naval aviation (SNA) has grown substantially over the last decade with the Crimean deployments of the TU–16 Badger (equipped with AS–5 and AS–6 surface-to-air missiles (SAM) and TU–22M Backfire bombers (equipped with AS–4 SAMs). This air threat requires that NATO pay greater attention to theater air defense and increase its efforts at modernizing land-based air assets in the region.

The increasing SNA threat (combined with the reduction of U.S. carriers permanently attached to the Sixth Fleet) would complicate efforts by the Sixth Fleet to assist NATO ground forces in a defensive battle with Warsaw Pact troops. Air superiority over the Mediterranean and its littorals would be a first priority followed by sea control. In sum, NATO's ability to "influence" the course of a southern flank land battle will be greatly reduced if the Sixth Fleet's strength is reduced again to only 1 carrier.

Should Soviet air and naval forces erode the U.S. naval tactical air umbrella in the eastern Mediterranean, effective synergistic operations with land-based tactical air assets in Turkey and Greece would become impossible. Although an effective, coordinated Soviet attack would have to include long-range bombers, antiship missiles, and submarine-launched missiles, a three-pronged attack is within the realm of current Soviet capability. Preparation for such an attack would, however, give some strategic warning to NATO. Moreover, an attack on the Sixth Fleet would escalate the conflict immediately and raise the threshold of a limited operation beyond the point where Soviet planners might be prepared to go.

Naval Crisis Management

From the standpoint of U.S.-Soviet or NATO–Warsaw Pact crisis management, air and naval forces in the Mediterranean would probably be the key factor in most contingencies. For this reason the Soviet naval buildup in the Mediterranean is most troubling. Dramatic increases in numbers of combatants occurred during the 1967 and 1973 Arab-Israeli wars. The 1967 case marked the first time the Soviets employed a large naval force in the Third World during a crisis.[24] This force, however, was inferior to that of the Sixth Fleet at that time.

The Jordanian crisis marked the second such Soviet deployment. During September and October 1970 the size of the Fifth Escadra increased from 46 to 60 ships; major surface combatants rose steadily from 8 ships.[25] This case is particularly relevant for this study, as it illustrates the dynamic relationship between internal political stresses and foreign policy in the southern region. During the Jordanian crisis the probability that the United States would not be able to make use of Greek and Turkish bases in any Mediterranean operations weighed heavily in the JCS assessment of the situation.[26] At a meeting of the JCS on September 11, 1970, the importance of base rights in Turkey was made obvious when it was suggested that the United States might be forced to land an army brigade to secure these bases prior to any landing.[27]

It was considered axiomatic that the NATO political leadership would not endorse a U.S. military initiative in the Mediterranean in support of the besieged Jordanian government. It was also obvious to all those involved in this crisis that the Turkish and Greek governments would find it difficult to withstand the public outcry against allowing their soil to be used as a staging area for U.S. troops. Finally, the JCS could not be certain that Turkey would close the straits to Soviet ships in any crisis, despite Turkey's responsibility under the Montreux Convention for the security of the straits.

The October 1973 Arab-Israeli War provides an instructive case study of crisis management in the Mediterranean. Of primary importance is the question of strategic warning. It is clear now that the Soviets were informed directly by the Egyptians and the Syrians of an impending attack on Israeli forces. Although the length of strategic warning given the Soviets is uncertain, an examination of the timing of their naval reinforcement efforts in the Mediterranean suggests at least three weeks. The need to allow at least eight or nine days to reinforce the Fifth

Escadra with surface combatants from the Black Sea Fleet, the restrictions imposed by the Montreux Convention, and the longer period of time required for nuclear and conventional submarine reinforcement appear to have been taken into account during the crisis.

Soviet activity in the region was at a peak. Efforts were made to disarm any operation that distracted from the preparations for war with Israel (including the dispatch of naval chief Admiral Sergei Gorshkov and a small fleet to Iraq to oppose Iraqi seizure of Kuwaiti border territory). During the October war Soviet submarine reinforcement brought forces in the Mediterranean to the following levels: 25 attack submarines, 29 surface combatants, 8 amphibious ships and 36 intelligence-collection vessels and auxiliary ships.

The Sixth Fleet was also strengthened substantially with reinforcements, including the dispatch of a third carrier task group to the Mediterranean (to include the *FDR*, the *Independence*, and the *John F. Kennedy*) coincident with the DEFCON III alert.[28] The United States had substantial strategic warning and acted upon it early enough to shift naval forces in a timely fashion.

Apart from the usual accounts of the war, several observations can be made at this point: (1) the Montreux Convention did affect Soviet reinforcement capability, (2) the Soviets were aware that in order to reduce U.S. naval capability in the Mediterranean seriously, the three U.S. carriers would have to be targeted (the escalation risks in such a strategy are obvious), and (3) the Soviets were generally cautious in their behavior during the October war, although their deployment appeared to be more than the usual posturing. At one point the Soviet fleet was interposed between the U.S. Sixth Fleet and the Syrian/Egyptian coastline—a deployment fraught with the possibilities for a U.S.-Soviet confrontation. It was largely because the Soviets realized the extent of the U.S. commitment to Israel that the danger was contained. The risks might have increased substantially, however, if the war had been prolonged.

Fleet Protection

Problems of fleet defense in open-ocean areas are not substantially different from those in enclosed bodies of water such as the Mediterranean. The Sixth Fleet operating in the eastern Mediterranean in a conflict situation would be vulnerable—as noted earlier—to attack from both bombers and fighters of extended range and high performance based in the Crimea and Bulgaria. Bombers carrying AS–4, AS–5, and AS–6 missiles could attack along any azimuth. Depending on the carrier task force's location, long-range Soviet fighters could have a similar capability. The vulnerability of an aircraft carrier is multiplied whenever it is utilized as the primary platform for offshore naval power projection. As noted earlier, this is because the primary mission for carrier-based aircraft is to protect the carrier, which leaves relatively few planes available for a power-projection role mission. Therefore such an operation should utilize both land-based and sea-based assets, where available.

The proximity of allied territory, however, makes it possible to consider use of facilities ashore to base allied or U.S. naval or air-force fighters as well as airborne warning and control system aircraft (AWACS) in support of the fleet. AWACS and fighters based in Turkey, for example, could

- Increase jam-resistant early warning for the Sixth Fleet, allowing more time for the U.S. carrier force in the eastern Mediterranean to launch interceptors; and,
- Provide an effective layer of air defense for Turkey as well as for the U.S. fleet.

For any significant improvement in eastern Mediterranean/southern flank air defense, the Turkish and Greek governments would have to make available additional airfields, and NATO air-defense ground environment (NADGE) sites would have to be upgraded significantly. Greek-Turkish cooperation is essential if the NADGE network is to function as an integrated net, however, the prospects for such cooperation are bleak. The deployment of AWACS would then become more critical, since Greece and Turkey could control separate AWACS orbits (although this would obviously not be the most efficient utilization of a scarce resource). The entire NATO airborne early warning E–3A force will consist of only 18 aircraft. A number of Nimrods will also be operated by the British as part of this force.

Depending on the contingency, Israeli airfields could play a vital role in a U.S.-Soviet conflict in the southern region. Obviously, this would require a political decision by the Israeli government. Although U.S.-Israeli strategic cooperation was seriously discussed between the two governments in the early period of the first Reagan administration, the Israeli invasion of Lebanon and tension over the Israeli settlement policy in the West Bank substantially cooled U.S. enthusiasm for such discussions. In light of more recent developments, however, rapprochement between Tel Aviv and Washington has led to a reopening of these talks.

The U.S. Sixth Fleet is in a paradoxical position. In the event of a Soviet attack its survival is doubtful, but its continued presence does provide an effective deterrent in crisis situations, as illustrated by Soviet behavior in several cases described above. In a Mediterranean Sea war, the U.S. carriers and other allied carriers would be priority targets; unless reinforced substantially beyond the current level, they would be early casualties of Soviet naval and air bombardment. Without substantially improved land-based air protection from Greece and Turkey the carriers could not adequately defend themselves, let alone project power ashore.

Unless the U.S. Navy is prepared to augment the "permanent" Mediterranean deployment of 2 carriers, the full deterrent force of the Sixth Fleet will not be realized. In addition, the navy should consider more frequent surge exercises in the Mediterranean that bring the total carrier force there up to 3 or 4 carrier-battle groups. Finally, preparations for alternative anchorages for the Sixth Fleet should be considered in the event that U.S. bases in Greece are dismantled in 1988.

4.
THE DEFENSE SITUATION IN THE SOUTHERN REGION

Geographical Constraints on Strategy

Geographical factors make a cohesive defense on the southern flank difficult. Italy is cut off from NATO's central region by France, Switzerland, and Austria. Nonaligned Yugoslavia stands between Greece and Italy. The Caucasus region to the east of Turkey is far removed from the bulk of NATO forces. Geographically separated land combat areas and the need to defend national frontiers dictates that, at least initially, battles would be fought almost exclusively by national forces in defense of national soil—a very different situation from that found in central Europe. U.S. air and naval power would play a role assuming sufficient warning, political will, and a timely decision by Washington to allocate forces.

As noted earlier, the constraining geography combined with Greek-Turkish differences make mutual support among the combat areas extremely difficult. Shifting forces, including the more flexible air forces, will be problematical, as the current infrastructure requires modernization. Base capacity on the southern flank (and in ACE generally) is limited. There are, however, certain advantages on NATO's side. Yugoslavia's nonaligned status means that any Warsaw Pact attack toward Italy or through the most favored approaches through northern Greece would provide some strategic warning. In addition, it is likely that Yugoslavian forces would act to repel a Soviet attack. Furthermore, for the Soviets to be in a position to attack in the area of Thrace (and northern Greece) toward the Turkish straits, they would have to transit Romania and Bulgaria—again providing strategic warning. At the extreme eastern end of Turkey, Turkish and Soviet forces directly confront each other on land, where warning (communicated through the movement of opposing forces) would be minimal.

Yugoslavia could play a key role in NATO's ability to prepare a defense on the southern flank. It is unclear, however, how the Yugoslav leadership would weigh the risks to its own security in deciding whether to assist NATO in stalling a Warsaw Pact attack. Clearly, this decision would be scenario-dependent. While the Yugoslavs might cooperate in providing base access to Western forces in the event of a Middle Eastern contingency, a Warsaw Pact attack on Europe would present Belgrade with a critical test of its nonaligned status. Although Yugoslavia's geographical proximity to the Soviet Union dictates caution by Belgrade, confidential discussions between the United States and Yugoslavia over base access could produce private understandings similar to those that exist with other non-NATO states.

The late Yugoslav leader, Marshal Tito, was not always willing to assist the West during periods of crisis. During the 1973 Arab-Israeli War, for example, Tito allowed Moscow to use Yugoslav facilities and airspace to fly military supplies to Egypt. Although the decision was probably more a function of Tito's sympathy for the Arab cause, the result was assistance of Soviet forces in a wartime situation. Tito's attitude toward Moscow was inconsistent, however. In 1976 he refused a request from Leonid Brezhnev to allow an increase in the servicing of Soviet warships in Yugoslav ports. Post-Tito policy toward Moscow or the West is more difficult to gauge, since few situations have tested the policy. Yugoslav ports could be used to service allied naval units, reducing the home-port time required. In addition, cooperation by the Yugoslav military in areas like air defense would increase tactical warning for the southern region, although the prospects for military talks between Washington and Belgrade are not promising.

Southern Flank Military Balance

The salient features of the military balance in the three land theaters (excluding Iberia) are as follows:[29]

Northern Greece/Turkish Thrace. The Warsaw Pact could commit 34 Soviet, Romanian, and Bulgarian divisions to a contingency in this theater. These forces are largely mechanized and are equipped with a total of 6,750 tanks and nearly 6,500 artillery and mortar pieces. The terrain is eminently suitable for armored offensive operations and could be reinforced by amphibious forces and by the equivalent of 3 divisions of airborne, air mobile, and air assault troops. According to the 1984 NATO–Warsaw Pact force comparison study, of the 34 Pact divisions available for a contingency in this theater, 22 are either deployed forward or in a "high state of readiness."

Non-Soviet Warsaw Pact troops committed to this theater would be drawn from the southwestern theater of military operations, one of three theaters in the Western strategic theater. Soviets troops would be drawn from the Carpathian and Odessa military districts (MDs). Soviet forces from the Kiev MD could reinforce these units.

By comparison, Greek and Turkish divisions deployable for combat in this theater number 25. They are mainly infantry, vastly outnumbered, and poorly equipped. Greek and Turkish land forces are shown in tables 4 and 5; air forces, in tables 6 and 7.

Eastern Turkey. Available for combat in this theater are 20 Soviet divisions, equipped with 4,300 tanks and nearly 5,000 artillery pieces. Of this force, roughly 12 divisions (including 2,435 tanks and 2,735 artillery and mortar pieces) are forward deployed. As with Soviet troops in Thrace, these forces could also be reinforced by air-assault/mobile divisions and by amphibious forces. There would be some overlap between these forces and those committed to the Thrace theater.

Soviet forces committed to a campaign in eastern Turkey would include units from two MDs—Transcaucasus and North Caucasus. Reinforcements could be deployed from the Odessa or Volga MDs.

NATO forces in this theater are limited to 8 Turkish divisions in the northeastern portion of the country. Four additional divisions deployed in the southeast protect Turkey's border but could be moved northward for reinforcement if necessary. There is some overlap between Soviet forces available in Thrace and in eastern Turkey.

Northern Italy. The Warsaw Pact has 10 Soviet and Hungarian divisions, equipped with roughly 2,500 tanks and 1,600 artillery pieces that could be used in this theater. These divisions, located in Hungary, could be reinforced by 7 more divisions equipped with 2,000 tanks and 1,300 artillery pieces from the Kiev MD. According to the 1984 NATO–Warsaw Pact force comparison study, however, these 7 divisions are not rated category 1—that is, they are at least 25 percent understrength and inadequately equipped.

NATO land forces in this theater are limited to 4 Italian divisions and 12 independent brigades, including some 1,250 tanks and 1,400 artillery and mortar pieces. Forces in this theater are deployed in 3 corps. In addition, Portugal provides a reinforcement brigade for deployment in this theater.

The recent reorganization of the Soviet air forces into 20 regional commands and 5 air armies complicates an analysis of Soviet air assets that could be committed to a southern region conflict. In addition, Soviet air defense has also been reorganized, collapsing the 10 air-defense districts to 5.

The air balance in the southern region (assuming no major shift of forces) shows 615 fighter-bomber and ground-attack aircraft available to NATO against 695 for the Warsaw Pact. The interceptor asymmetry is significant, however, with NATO deploying 295 planes against 1,560 for the Warsaw Pact. In addition, the range of some of the more modern Soviet aircraft would allow coverage of the entire Mediterranean.

Italy: Stable but Weak

Italy's military contribution to NATO is often ignored or eclipsed by discussions of Turkish and Greek contributions. This is unfortunate, since Italy's military force is not insignificant (see Table 8).

Despite more than forty changes in government since the conclusion of World War II, virtually all postwar administrations in Rome have been strong supporters of NATO and of a strengthened capability in the south. Unfortunately, much of this support has been rhetorical rather than demonstrative. Italy's commitment to defense (measured in terms of percent of gross national product [GNP]) has actually declined, although Italy's ranking among NATO nations has remained constant. From 1971-83 Italy ranked eleventh in terms of GNP percentage committed to defense, at 2.7 percent. In active duty military manpower Italy ranks fifth, although there has been a 7.7 percent decline since 1971. In armored divisions equivalents it ranks as the seventh largest contributor. Its naval contribution is significant, and Italy's principal surface combatants rank fifth, just below those of Canada.[30] It also ranks fifth in terms of tactical combat aircraft (just above Turkey).

Italy's location in the center of the Mediterranean almost guarantees that in any NATO–Warsaw Pact naval engagement, Italian naval forces would become involved in the battle. The northern Italian theater is also critically situated and if overrun, would expose southern Germany and eastern France to Warsaw Pact air forces. Clearly, Italy's role would be critical in a military crisis, but Italian governments have declined to accept a larger role in southern region defense. Two key problems are a reduction in the size of Italy's armed forces (estimated at 385,000) and a lack of training.[31] Unless the Italian government is willing to increase significantly annual defense expenditures and NATO infrastructure contributions, Italy's role will continue to be discounted in the region's defense planning.

TABLE 4
Greek Land Combat Forces (1985–1986)

1 armored division	13 field artillery battalions
1 mechanized division	7 antiaircraft artillery battalions
11 infantry divisions	2 surface-to-surface missile battalions (Honest John)
1 parachute-commando division	2 surface-to-air missile battalions (Improved Hawk)
3 armored brigades	

TABLE 5
Turkish Land Combat Forces (1985–1986)

2 mechanized infantry divisions	11 infantry brigades
14 infantry divisions	1 parachute brigade
6 armored brigades	1 commando brigade
4 mechanized brigades	4 surface-to-surface missile battalions

TABLE 6
Greek Air Forces (1985–1986)

8 fighter ground-attack squadrons (A–7H, TA–7H, F/TF–104G, F–5A, F–5B)
6 interceptor squadrons (F–4E, F–5A/B, Mirage F–1CG)
2 reconnaissance squadrons (RF–84F, RF–4E, RF–5A)
3 transport squadrons (C–1300H, YS–11, C–47)
3 helicopter squadrons (AB–205A, AB–206A, Bell 47G, UH–19D, AB–212, CH–47C)
Air-to-air missiles (Sparrow, Sidewinder, Falcon)
Air-to-surface missiles (Maverick, Bullpup)
Surface-to-air missiles (Nike Ajax)

Sources: The Military Balance, 1984–1985, 1985–1986 (London: International Institute for Strategic Studies, 1984, 1985); John M. Collins, *U.S.–Soviet Military Balance, 1980–1985* (New York: Pergamon Brasseys, 1984); *NATO and the Warsaw Pact: Force Comparisons* (Brussels: NATO Information Service, 1984).

TABLE 7
Turkish Air Forces (1985–1986)

---

17 fighter ground-attack squadrons (F–5A, F–5B, F–100D, F–4E, F–104G, TF–104)
  2 interceptor squadrons (F–104, TF–104G)
  2 reconnaissance squadrons (RF–5A, F–5B, RF–4E)
  6 transport squadrons (C–130E, C–160D, C–47A)
  5 operational conversion units (F–5A/B, F–104G, T–33A, T–37C)
  3 training squadrons (T–34A, T–38A, T–41D)
Air-to-air missiles (Sidewinder, Sparrow, Falcon, Shafir)
Air-to-surface missiles (AS–12, Bullpup, Maverick)
Surface-to-air missiles (Nike Hercules, 2 Rapier squadrons forming)

Sources: The Military Balance, 1984–1985, 1985–1986 (London: International Institute for Strategic Studies, 1984, 1985); John M. Collins, U.S.–Soviet Military Balance, 1980–1985 (New York: Pergamon Brasseys, 1984); NATO and the Warsaw Pact: Force Comparisons (Brussels: NATO Information Service, 1984).

TABLE 8
Italian Combat Forces (Selected Indicators) (1985–1986)

Army

1 armored division (2 armored, 1 mechanized brigade)
3 mechanized divisions
2 independent mechanized brigades
4 independent motorized brigades
5 alpine brigades

Tanks: 500 M–47
      300 M–60 A1
      970 Leopard 1

Armored
Personnel : 4,110 – M–106
Carriers   M–113
           M–548
           M–577

Air Force

6 fighter ground-attack reconnaissance squadrons (F–104, Tornado)
6 tactical squadrons (MB–339, G91R)
7 fighter squadrons (F–104)
8 surface-to-air missile groups (Nike Hercules, Spada)

Navy

10 submarines
 1 helicopter carrier
 2 cruisers
 4 destroyers
16 frigates
 8 corvettes
 2 fast-attack craft
 2 amphibious ships
 5 antisubmarine squadrons

Sources: The Military Balance, 1984–1985, 1985–1986 (London: International Institute for Strategic Studies, 1984, 1985); Jane's Defense Weekly (1984–1985).

Note: This table presents a profile of military capability listing only those weapons and systems that the author regards as key indicators of military power.

The Reliability of Soviet Allies

A potentially significant factor in assessing Warsaw Pact strength in a southern flank contingency is the political reliability of non-Soviet Warsaw Pact forces.[32] Of the Soviet Union's three southern tier allies—Bulgaria, Hungary, and Romania—only the Bulgarian troops can be considered thoroughly reliable. Soviet planners regard the participation of Hungarian and Romanian troops as problematic. This is acknowledged by Romanian and Hungarian officials. Romanian officials acknowledged this during private talks with the author in Bucharest in 1983. Reportedly, the issue of political reliability, a constant irritant in Romanian-Soviet relations, was raised in 1983 by the Warsaw Pact commander in chief, Marshal Viktor Kulikov.

The issue of reliability would obviously affect Warsaw Pact force levels in a southern flank contingency. If one accepts the presumption that only Bulgarian troops could be counted upon to participate at full strength in a Soviet military initiative in the south, then all three of the Warsaw Pact orders of battle listed earlier are somewhat inflated. The reliability of Bulgarian troops is partly related to a territorial issue with historic antecedents. Bulgaria never recovered small sections of Macedonia (now in Greece and Yugoslavia) to the south and west. Irredentist claims continue to irritate relations between Sofia and Belgrade. Marshal Tito had sought to use the Macedonian issue as a wedge in his quest for a Balkan federation. Only after Tito's break with Moscow was the border sealed in an attempt to end Yugoslavian attempts to create a greater Macedonia.

Since 1965 the Romanians have not participated on any large scale in Warsaw Pact maneuvers, and since 1964 the Romanian leadership has opposed multinational Warsaw Pact maneuvers on the territory of any member state. It is also true, however, that the Romanian President Nicolae Ceauşescu has never suggested he was prepared to abandon the Warsaw Pact military structure. Nevertheless, Romanian troops lack intensive integrative training with Soviet and Pact forces, and as a result their training (and in many cases equipment) lags significantly behind those of either the Bulgarians or the Hungarians.

It seems reasonable to assume that regardless of the contingency (except one designed to counter a territorial threat to Romania) Romanian military participation in a Soviet attack is highly doubtful. Romania has distanced itself from Moscow's recent European initiatives (opposing, for example, the deployment of intermediate-range nuclear forces [INF]) and Ceauşescu's close relations with many Arab leaders suggests he would not react enthusiastically to Moscow's requests to support Soviet involvement in a Persian Gulf conflict. In addition, the Romanian government maintains good relations with Israel, making it unlikely that Bucharest's position in future Arab-Israeli conflicts will be anything other than neutral or nonaligned.

Hungary, which maintains the smallest military force in Eastern Europe, is alone among the three southern tier states in hosting a large contingent of Soviet troops—2 tank and 2 mechanized infantry divisions. Hungarian troops have participated in Warsaw Pact exercises since 1962 on Hungarian soil and the soil of other Warsaw Pact allies. In Hungary— unlike the situation in Romania—the military forces are under the direct command of a Soviet general. There is every reason to believe that Hungarian troops would respond to a Soviet order to support Moscow militarily in opposing either a NATO or non-NATO contingency.

The Range of Contingencies

There is a range of contingencies that might provoke conflict in the southern region. First, while the Soviet Union has invested heavily in military forces assigned to this region, NATO has not. Generally, as already noted, NATO planners envision a southern flank conflict only as part of a larger Soviet assault in central Europe. Thus, the southern flank may be seen as a theater of secondary importance to the Alliance in a European crisis. This judgment is, of course, scenario-dependent. As a result, SACEUR may be most reluctant to commit resources to this region if conflict breaks out on the central front or if such conflict appears likely.

The "central front bias" continues to operate as the predominant concept in NATO's contingency planning; it may dominate crisis management as well. The southern flank's location, adjacent to the Middle East and Persian Gulf regions, increases the likelihood that conflict in the flank theater will begin as a result of internal crises elsewhere and, more important, in regions designated as "out-of-area," that is, outside of NATO's formal treaty area. This perception has led southern flank states to remove themselves from any public discussion over U.S. power projection into the Persian Gulf region. These factors increase the likelihood that NATO will delay or refuse to deploy timely reinforcements to the region.

For reasons mentioned earlier, the concept of a "southern flank" is problematic. The term southern "flank," when used to refer to conflict in the NATO context, appears appropriate. In planning for the defense of the Mediterranean, however, it is perhaps more sensible to speak of the southern "region" to emphasize the role of the Mediterranean as a strategic link between Europe and the Middle East. While NATO's treaty boundaries do not extend to the Persian Gulf/Middle East, the Alliance's interests do, and these interests might be best served by a strategy that recognizes this fact. While the Persian Gulf/Middle East could never constitute a formal NATO command without a signficant amendment to and alteration of the North Atlantic Treaty (which would be inadvisable), a number of initiatives could be taken to link operationally these two theaters. For example, the current U.S. naval task force in the Indian Ocean could be augmented by units of allied navies without the formal NATO imprimatur. Allied naval exercises could be held in the Indian Ocean and Arabian Sea without formal concurrence of the NATO Council.

In sum, NATO members ought to develop a framework within which the Persian Gulf/Middle East is discussed regularly. (Western policy toward the gulf region is examined in Part 2 of this study.) Formally placing such issues on NATO council agendas is probably counterproductive. It is possible, however, to develop unofficial working groups of "interested" NATO states to deal with crises like the Iran-Iraq War and terrorism sponsored or supported by Mediterranean states.

At least seven discrete scenarios can be identified within a limitless range of contingencies in the southern region:

NATO CONTINGENCIES

CASE 1: A Soviet attack on the flank. NATO ministers promptly authorize an Alliance military response.

CASE 2: A Soviet attack on the flank. Some NATO ministers hesitate to authorize an Alliance military response for fear that assets will be moved prematurely before Soviet intent elsewhere in Europe is known (central front bias). The United States reacts unilaterally, sending troops and matériel.

CASE 3: A Soviet attack on the flank. The NATO council does not authorize an Alliance military response. The United States chooses (in the absence of any NATO response) not to respond unilaterally.

CASE 4: A European-wide NATO–Warsaw Pact war in which the southern flank is under attack along with the center and the northern flank. Reinforcements for the flank are not forthcoming due to commitments elsewhere.

NON-NATO CONTINGENCIES

CASE 5: A conflict in the Middle East erupts. Soviet forces intervene, some violating NATO airspace. Involvement of NATO forces is approved by the NATO council.

CASE 6: The Soviets become involved in an internal upheaval in one of the gulf states. The United States deploys the Rapid Deployment

Joint Task Force (RDJTF) to the Persian Gulf in response. Flank states are "dragged into" the conflict as a result of U.S. actions.

CASE 7: An Arab-Israeli war. Israel requests U.S. assistance. The Arab states appeal to the Soviet Union.

Cases 1 and 2 have several variants. A Soviet attack could be limited to the Thrace/straits region or to eastern Turkey. However, the terrain in eastern Turkey is forbidding and there would be no clear strategic reason for such a Soviet initiative. If Soviet access to the Persian Gulf is the goal, an attack through Iran might be a more attractive option. It is also unlikely that the Soviets would attack in both theaters simultaneously, since this would split their forces and prolong the battle. In addition, a Soviet attempt to present NATO with a fait accompli by attacking in a very limited theater such as the Thrace/straits region before NATO is able to energize its political decisionmaking machinery may appear to be a lower risk option than either a wider attack on NATO or an attack in another theater on the flank such as eastern Turkey or northern Italy. This would be particularly true if the Soviets prepositioned sufficient forces to accomplish their objective quickly. Furthermore, the southern flank is a region where military policy may dictate caution (derived in part from a concern that interests in "primary" areas not be sacrificed for the flank), where rapid reinforcement is problematic at best, and where such internal disputes as that between Greece and Turkey threaten to prevent effective command and control in wartime (as they have in recent exercises).

Three points should be made concerning a Thrace/straits scenario. First, from NATO's perspective the strategic requirement is to hold the Turkish straits (the Bosporus and the Dardanelles) and thus deny the Soviet navy transit to and from the Black Sea. Should control of the straits be lost to a Soviet invasion, a defense in the Aegean would still be possible, utilizing naval and air power. Such a strategy emphasizes the necessity to hold Crete.

Second, there is little in depth defense on land in this theater. In both northern Greece and Turkish Thrace suitable defensive positions hardly exist, except for the mountain passes on the Greek-Bulgarian border. Allied positions would probably be overrun very quickly without early reinforcements.

Third, an attack would probably occur along with a U.S.-Soviet naval campaign in the Mediterranean. This would strain current NATO naval assets, as there might be two simultaneous naval battles, each competing for the same resources. Seizing the straits would represent a signficant military gain for the Soviets, while the political cost would be catastrophic for NATO.

A Soviet military initiative in eastern Turkey (as a variant of either Case 1, 2, or 3) would present a different set of conditions for the Alliance. The territory in this theater is forbidding but historically attractive to the Soviets, as it was when they attempted to annex a portion of it immediately following World War II. In addition to inciting an uprising of the resident Kurdish population (as analyst Paul Henze has shown, the Soviet Union has attempted to destabilize this portion of Turkey by transmitting anti-Turkish broadcasts from Eastern Europe), an attack into eastern Turkey would bring the Soviets appreciably closer to the Persian Gulf, particularly if the attack occurred simultaneously with a Soviet attack on Iran. An attack against Iran would allow the Soviets to achieve a goal that holds historic attraction for Moscow— Iranian Azerbaijan.

Finally, a number of sensitive U.S. surveillance facilities are located in eastern Turkey. The value of these installations has been significantly increased as a result of the loss of similar stations in Iran. These facilities might pose attractive targets for a Soviet invasion force.

In sum, Case 1, 2 and 3 assume—in varying degrees—that the Soviet Union would be willing to risk a NATO response for a small military gain but a large political victory. They would also be gambling that NATO would either respond slowly or not at all to such an operation. Case 3 would represent the total political breakdown of NATO, presumably the ultimate Soviet goal. A decision by the United States and NATO not to respond to a Soviet attack within NATO territory is a rejection of the security covenant that supports the Alliance itself. Yet it is not implausible to suggest that an attack on Turkey or other southern flank nations would fail to galvanize NATO or the United States to respond militarily.

Of the non-NATO contingencies Case 6 appears to be the most likely. While the United States would be reluctant to commit forces to the Middle East prematurely, the threatened stability of moderate and pro-Western states in the region—such as Saudi Arabia, Kuwait, and Oman— would warrant such a commitment, particularly if the Soviet Union had already deployed forces to the area. It is unlikely, however, that the NATO council could be persuaded that a NATO deployment could be justified (Case 5) in terms of political cost or even military prudence.

Although in many ways European interests (particularly in the economic sphere) are more directly at stake in a Middle Eastern conflict than U.S. interests, the European allies have been most reluctant to acknowledge that fact publicly. In addition, European leaders are suspicious of U.S. motivations in the region, which to Europeans often seem to derive from an exaggerated U.S. concern over the potential for Soviet exploitation of, or participation in, an internal crisis. In sum, the European reaction would differ according to the scenario.

In the event of an Arab-Israeli conflict (Case 7) a direct threat to European *economic* interests is much less likely unless the Soviet Union attempts to seize the oil fields, which would be unlikely in the context of an Arab-Israeli war. The involvement of outside powers in an Arab-Israeli conflict is likely to be limited to the two superpowers, as demonstrated in 1967 and 1973. That involvement (at least in the initial stages) would most probably be confined to resupply of regional clients and allies.

A U.S. decision to deploy elements of the RDJTF *effectively* would require cooperation by both Middle Eastern allies and NATO allies for base access and overflight. Unless the NATO allies could be persuaded that the crisis represented a severe and direct threat to their interests, the Europeans would be unlikely to grant such assistance. This would not, however, restrict such Middle Eastern allies as Israel and such friendly states as Oman and Saudi Arabia from assisting in a U.S. interventionary effort. The constraints in this case would be primarily related to regime concerns about a close identification with U.S. policy in the region.

Overflight: Political and Military Aspects

Political sensitivities and military capabilities could be tested without the occurrence of actual armed conflict. Such might be the case during a crisis if the Soviet Union was to overfly the territory of a NATO ally as part of an operation to support regional surrogates in the Middle East. Should the Soviet government decide to overfly Greece and Turkey or notify Athens and Ankara of their intention to do so, it is unclear how the two governments would respond. These nations control the most direct air route from the borders of the Warsaw Pact to the Middle East, and they, particularly Greece under Papandreou, might find the pressure to grant overflight too great to endure.

Overflight could be a critical issue in Soviet attempts to resupply such regional allies as Syria. Considering the antiquated state of their air defenses, neither Turkey nor Greece is capable of enforcing a denial of overflight should the Soviet Union choose to test matters. Whether NATO and/or the United States would consider guaranteeing reinforcement in the event that either country choses to challenge a Soviet decision to overfly (and whether the Greek and Turkish governments would consider such guarantees credible) is equally debatable. This should not be a matter of choice for NATO, however.

A violation of NATO airspace by the Soviet Union should activate the NATO guarantee to protect the sovereignty of a member state. A NATO refusal to respond to such a violation would essentially be a decision to ignore the collective defense obligations of the Alliance. However, in the 1973 Arab-Israeli War the Soviets persuaded Yugoslavia to cooperate while the United States failed to prevail upon Greece and Turkey to allow access to bases. In the final analysis, strengthening air defenses in Greece and Turkey should be a high priority for both governments and for NATO.

Problems of Command and Control

As referred to elsewhere in this study, no other region in Allied Command Europe suffers from such a complex and disjointed command network. Although C^2 is a problem throughout NATO, the geographical and political complexities in the southern flank are unique in Europe. No other region has such a multiplicity of headquarters at so many levels. There are functional and area commands at both the principal subordinate command and the subordinate levels. In addition, relocation of headquarters in wartime presents particular difficulties, since in many cases the wartime headquarters will have housed national headquarters in peacetime.

Warning and Surveillance

The NATO alert system would be tested most severely in the event of a southern flank crisis. NATO's formal alert system is a sluggish network of formal procedures by means of which national forces are transferred to NATO commands. There are essentially two sets of alert measures: a graduated series of measures used when considerable warning is available, and a more rapid set of procedures when a surprise attack has actually occurred. As is well known, NATO has limited warning capability of its own (excluding the rather antiquated NADGE system). In peacetime, intelligence collection is primarily by national forces, transmitted to Supreme Headquarters, Allied Powers Europe (SHAPE). If warning indicates that a stage of alert is required, SACEUR must consult with the members of the NATO council and its Defense Planning Committee prior to issuance of the alert. Quite obviously, procedural mechanisms will be followed with greater caution as NATO moves closer to a wartime situation. Political issues will determine the rapidity of action, not simply whether the system is "streamlined." There is some flexibility in the system. SACEUR, for example, does have the ability to generate certain forces (after presidential authorization) in his capacity as the U.S. commander in Europe (CINCEUR), independent of NATO channels.

Although all member nations have the ability to generate such actions, the U.S. role would obviously be special and would act as a signal to other major NATO states in the event of a crisis. This would be particularly critical in the southern region. It is unclear whether Greek and Turkish forces would respond with the same level of concern to Soviet troop, naval, or air movements. In this case, the U.S. response would be the key factor in determining the postures of regional states. The United States would consequently face a dilemma. A preemptive (and unilateral) U.S. military action might be resented by Greece and Turkey, who would consider the response premature and, therefore, an action that might inhibit subsequent military action by Athens and Ankara. On the other hand, the other NATO allies would read U.S. hesitancy as a signal that an attack on the southern flank did not represent a major threat to the Alliance as a whole and that the southern region itself was not regarded by the United States as strategically significant enough to activate the NATO guarantee.

Surveillance of airspace is a critical part of warning. NATO has acquired 18 E–3A aircraft for this purpose. In addition, 11 British Nimrod aircraft would contribute to the NATO Airborne Early Warning (AEW) Force, although these aircraft would probably be limited to surveillance of the waters surrounding Great Britain. NATO AEW aircraft flying at 30,000 feet should be able to detect flying targets at ranges up to about 400 kilometers. The situation would change radically in wartime, however, when these aircraft would be forced to operate further back to avoid Warsaw Pact interceptors and ground-based jammers. Although the 400-kilometer area sounds impressive, it is actually quite small in comparison to the vast area of the southern region and the many air approaches along the front. A large number of AEW aircraft would be required to cover the entire region, considering that 4 to 5 aircraft are needed to maintain continuous coverage. This would be further strained in a crisis that developed in the Persian Gulf by the necessity to monitor air corridors to the southern flank and the Middle East simultaneously.

Finally, maritime surveillance would be critical in the southern region, where a body of water—the Mediterranean—links several separated land theaters. Certain flank states may be hesitant about monitoring Soviet naval traffic in areas other than those adjacent to territorial waters. As the eastern Mediterranean provides a Soviet maritime route to the Persian Gulf, a particularly wide arc of surveillance would be required. U.S. ships would probably have to assume the larger part of the burden.

There is an obvious need for improved surveillance in the Mediterranean. A number of steps have been taken to strengthen NATO's capability, including a 1984 reaffirmation by the Papandreou government to accept 1 AWACS aircraft to be based at the Greek air-force base at Prevenza on the western Ionian Sea coast.[33] Ground radar facilities are being upgraded to enable a link with the aircraft. The Greek decision is significant, since the original commitment was made by the conservative predecessor government. The E–3A surveillance orbit will concentrate on Greece's northern border with Bulgaria. The AWACS deployment in Greece is part of a NATO-wide effort to establish a network of forward-operating bases (FOB) for the E–3A. The Greek decision will complete a southern flank AWACS network of three FOB locations at Konya, Turkey; Trapani, Italy; and Prevenza, Greece.

Apart from the AWACS deployment it is unclear whether the Alliance will be willing to commit the funds necessary to upgrade significantly NATO early warning and surveillance capabilities in the region. The AWACS deployment does provide an important component, but serious gaps in coverage (particularly the low-level air threat) remain. Until a decision is made to address this problem, southern flank forces (including the Sixth Fleet) will remain vulnerable to a short-warning Soviet attack.

5.
TURKEY'S CRITICAL ROLE

A Delicate Balancing Act

Turkey is of obvious importance to the defense of the southern region. It is one of only two NATO members (the other being Norway) to share a border with the Soviet Union. In addition to control of naval traffic through the Bosporus and Dardanelles, Turkey has potential control of the vital airspace in the region, and is ideally located to assume a role in any Persian Gulf contingency. The record of U.S.-Turkish relations since the Truman Doctrine has been incongruent. Indeed, that relationship has been mercurial. At the height of this strategic partnership in the 1950s Turkey proved to be a valuable ally in the United States' effort in the Korean War, allowing the construction of twenty-six U.S. military bases on Turkish soil, including major installations and intelligence-gathering facilities.

The situation changed radically in 1958 when the U.S. utilized Turkey as a staging area for its intervention in the Lebanon crisis. Lebanon had requested U.S. assistance after the fall of the Iraqi monarchy that year. The use of Turkish bases by the United States without permission of the Turkish government greatly angered the Turks, who resented being used as a client state. This incident is regarded by many as a turning point in U.S.-Turkish relations.[34]

In 1960 the first of three Turkish military coups gave the Soviets one of many opportunities to suggest that Turkey adopt a more "neutral" stance in foreign policy and leave the NATO Alliance, which it had joined only eight years earlier. To create tensions between Ankara and Washington—a long-time Soviet goal—Soviet premier Nikita Khrushchev wrote to the Turkish premier seeking to link Turkey's exit from NATO to the legacy of Kemal Atatürk, the architect of Turkish independence. The letter stated in part:

If the new Turkish government really abides by the policy of Atatürk, we shall all see Soviet-Turkish relations return to the high level of good-neighborliness and genuine friendship, which existed during the days of V.I. Lenin and the leader of the new Turkey, Atatürk.[35]

Turkish-Soviet relations had become inflamed over the 1959 deployment of Jupiter IRBMs in Turkey, a deployment the Soviet Union considered provocative. Writing in the Soviet journal, *International Affairs*, Kh. Grigoryan declared that the Jupiter deployment would create "a national danger for Turkey herself first and foremost" and argued against Turkey's increasing military and economic dependency on "U.S. imperialism."[36] In February 1962 the Soviet naval chief, Admiral Sergei Gorshkov, warned Turkey that the Jupiter missiles might provoke a Soviet attack that would "raze to the ground the countries adjacent to the Black Sea which have become NATO military bridge-heads."[37]

Twenty years later Soviet writers were still emphasizing the costs of Turkey's alliance with the United States and NATO, while recognizing Turkey's value to the West:

Progressive youth and women's organizations, the Society of Champions of Peace and all patriotically-minded Turkish citizens are enhancing the struggle for Turkey's peaceful development, against the country's becoming an outpost and nuclear testing ground of U.S. imperialism in the Middle East, against its participation in the imperialist NATO bloc.

. . . The people's mounting protest is alarming U.S. imperialist circles, who have long begun to regard Turkey as their military springboard near the Soviet frontier and the oil producing Mideast countries. The Republic of Turkey is merely NATO's southeastern flank, valued for its important strategic position.[38]

Soviet policy toward Turkey has included components that may at first seem to be contradictory. The Soviet Union has invested heavily in the social destabilization of Turkey's population, while simultaneously underwriting the construction of Turkish steel mills, cement factories, and aluminum plants. By 1978 Turkey had become the largest single recipient of Soviet aid among semi-industrialized states.[39] In addition, in late 1978 the governments of Turkey and the Soviet Union signed a three-year trade pact, which included a Soviet promise to provide roughly 25 percent of Turkey's petroleum supplies.[40]

Moscow is primarily interested in separating Turkey from NATO. That strategic objective is to be accomplished by pursuing policies that appear contradictory but are in fact complementary. Activities designed to advance these policies include: (1) threats to continue to mount a vast propaganda program to exacerbate the already acute, historically rooted tensions that exist between various segments of Turkey's socially heterogenous populace,[41] and (2) creation of a climate for détente between Moscow and Ankara by offering a program of economic aid through credit and grant programs far more attractive than any comparable efforts of Western institutions (for example, the European Economic Community [EEC], the World Bank, or NATO). Securing credit from these and other western leaders has proven increasingly difficult for Turkey. Because alternative sources of credit in the West are lacking and because it wishes to curtail Western control over its economic recovery program, the Turkish government has often responded favorably to Soviet offers.

Soviet arguments for a close relationship between Moscow and Ankara have looked quite attractive to Turkey, particularly during periods of strain in U.S.-Turkish relations. This strain has often been caused by rather callous and insensitive U.S. policy decisions. Prominent among these actions was the removal of Jupiter missiles in Turkey and the way in which president Lyndon B. Johnson handled the 1964 Cyprus crisis. President John F. Kennedy's assurances to Soviet premier Khrushchev that the United States would remove its Jupiter missiles from Turkey in exchange for removal of Soviet missiles from Cuba caused Turkey to question seriously the viability of its position in the Alliance. In addition, the sudden removal of these missiles signaled to some that Washington had concluded that the threat to Turkey was now somewhat reduced. A review of foreign-policy pronouncements subsequent to this episode reveals subtle but distinct changes in Turkey's attitude toward the Soviet Union. Shortly after the announcement that the IRBMs would be removed, Ankara signed a number of bilateral agreements with the Kremlin and—for the first time since 1932—sent a high-level parliamentary delegation to Moscow.[42]

Of equal concern to the Turks was a 1964 note from president Johnson to Turkish premier Ismet İnönü during the Cyprus crisis. Johnson warned İnönü that Turkey's NATO allies "have not had a chance to consider whether they have an obligation to protect Turkey against the Soviet Union if Turkey takes a step which results in Soviet intervention without the full consent and understanding of its NATO Allies."[43] Johnson also raised the question of utilizing NATO equipment for such a mission, and he specifically stated that "the United States cannot agree to the use of any United States supplied military equipment for a Turkish intervention in Cyprus under present circumstances."[44]

The most often cited example of Turkey's more independent stance toward the United States and NATO is the 1978 address by then–Turkish prime minister Bülent Ecevit to the International Institute for Strategic Studies in London. Ecevit clearly stated that Turkey's contribution to the Alliance in the future would depend on NATO's consideration of

Turkish security concerns. In addition, he made clear that continued use of U.S. military installations in Turkey would depend in part on the extent of U.S. long-term economic assistance for the ailing Turkish economy.[45] Finally, in 1979 Turkey informed the United States that in the future any flights of U-2 aircraft over Turkey for the purpose of monitoring Soviet compliance with SALT II could occur only with Soviet approval.[46] Overflight of Turkey has other vital aspects, including use of Turkish airspace for Middle Eastern contingencies and U.S. access to Turkish air bases.

Turkish reluctance to allow its facilities to be utilized in a Middle Eastern contingency is related to Turkish policies toward the Arab states. Determined efforts to be accepted by the states of the Arab Middle East since the 1960s reflect Ankara's historic dilemma of political and religious identification. On the one hand, Turkey has labored to be accepted as a Western state, with security concerns embodied in NATO membership. On the other hand, Islamic ties to the Arab world have prescribed a policy that at least questions the utility of a strong Western allegiance.

Geography has also dictated a special role for Turkey, which has both strategic advantages and socioreligious liabilities. Turkey's vital role as NATO's southeastern anchor tends to exacerbate the difficulty in becoming accepted in the Arab world, where suspicions of Western "hegemony" could be fueled by the image of a Turkish Trojan horse in the Middle East. Turkey's occasional attacks on militant Islam and Kemal Atatürk's drive to Westernize Turkey only fueled the Arab world's concern that while Ankara strove for acceptance by the fraternity of Arab states, Turkey was ultimately a Western nation, led by those who tied the country's security to the United States and NATO, not to the Arab world.

The national preoccupations and central concerns of Arab states as opposed to those of Turkey were far apart in the 1950s and 1960s, and specific policy issues increased the divergence. For the Arab states the nearly constant conflict—armed and otherwise—with Israel assumed paramount importance, while Turkey was consumed with stabilizing its position in the West. Policy toward Israel, however, became a perennial sticking point with Arab states, reminding Turkish leaders that while Ankara had originally opposed the partition of Palestine, it was the first Moslem country to recognize the new state of Israel, in 1949. Turkish-Israeli relations soured during the 1970s and early 1980s but have improved recently with the decision by both governments to upgrade the level of diplomatic representation at their respective embassies.

Relations with Israel suffered due to the 1975 decision by the Turkish government to establish bilateral relations with the Palestine Liberation Organization (PLO). This was sealed in 1979 when Turkey formally recognized the PLO as the legitimate representative of the Palestinian people. The recognition is understandable in the context of Turkish-Arab relations but very curious in the context of domestic stability in Turkey. The PLO has openly financed the Armenian terror network in Turkey and has publicly criticized Turkey's position on the Armenian question.

The OPEC oil embargo of 1973–74 shifted Turkey's foreign-policy emphasis from a course of cautious political dialogue with the Arab world to one of economic necessity. Turkey's dependence on OPEC petroleum demanded a closer relationship with key Persian Gulf and Middle Eastern oil exporters—Saudi Arabia, Kuwait, and Libya. At the same time, Turkey hoped both to increase its trade with the Middle Eastern countries and to attract petrodollars into the then seriously ailing Turkish economy.

Three Arab states—Libya, Syria, and Iraq—have particularly close relations with Turkey. The much publicized gift of 5 combat aircraft from Libya to Turkey during the 1974 Cyprus crisis was a tangible symbol of the attempt by Libyan head of state Muammar al-Qaddafi to move closer to Turkey. Although Turkey's friendly policy toward Libya is rooted primarily in economic concerns, there are other dimensions to that relationship. There is, for example, a strong and enduring guest-worker relationship between Libya and Turkey; roughly 10 percent of Turkey's expatriate workers in the Middle East live in Libya.

Turkish-Iraqi relations have also improved, mainly due to economic necessity. President Saddam Hussein's support for an oil pipeline from Mosul to Iskenderun, completed in 1977, proved vital to Turkey during the second oil shock of 1979. The issue of Kurdish separatism, however, remains a source of friction between the two states.

Turkey will continue to strive for a balanced policy that allows it to cater to both Western and Middle Eastern interests. That necessity for balance will inevitably create friction between Ankara and other NATO capitals. As a result, Turkey will always appear to be a "partial" member of NATO in terms of political allegiance. The inevitable pull toward the Middle East will continue and reduce the credibility of Turkey's insistence that it be "treated like a European state," even as it insists that NATO recognize its status as NATO's only Moslem member with strong links to the Arab world.

Since the bloodless military coup in Turkey in September 1980, Turkey's policy toward the United States specifically and toward NATO generally has changed considerably. Washington was clearly more comfortable with General Kenan Evren's National Security Council government than with Bülent Ecevit's Republican People's party. There was, however, some ambivalence due to the nature of the Ankara regime.

This attitude was captured during congressional testimony shortly after the September coup, when assistant secretary of state for European affairs George Vest appeared before Congressman Lee Hamilton's subcommittee on European and Middle Eastern affairs:

> *Mr. Hamilton:* Mr. Secretary. Are we pleased with the takeover by the military in Turkey?
>
> *Mr. Vest:* Pleased is the wrong verb, sir.
>
> *Mr. Hamilton:* We are not pleased?
>
> *Mr. Vest:* I would not say I am pleased and I would not say I am not pleased. I think I should say I understand what it is that has driven the Turkish military within the history of Turkey.[47]

Regardless of how one evaluates the effect of a military government within the Alliance, the result was clear. The political terrorism that had ravaged the country stopped, and an impressive economic recovery began. Since the extent of Turkey's internal difficulties will affect its contribution to NATO, one should not hastily condemn the Turkish military, which has kept its original pledge to return the country to democratic rule.

Return to Democracy

After more than three years of military government Turkey returned to democratic rule in December 1983. The five-man military junta (the National Security Council), which had ruled since September 1980, dissolved itself, allowing its leader, General Evren (who served as the council chief and the country's president), to remain as president for six more years. In addition, the National Security Council, although officially dissolved, was reconstituted as the Presidential Council.[48] In the Presidential Council the military has created a mechanism to monitor the progress of the civilian leadership.

Leading the new Turkish government is Prime Minister Turgut Özal, who founded a new political party—the Motherland party—to challenge the election slate favored by General Evren and the military, the Nationalist Democracy party. The Motherland party (one of three political parties allowed to participate in the elections) captured 212 seats in the 400-seat parliament. Özal had served as deputy prime minister in the Evren government and as economics minister in the administration of Suleyman Demirel. He was also the chief architect of economic reform and growth in Turkey. In becoming prime minister he replaced a retired admiral, Bülent Ulusu, who had served on the five-man National Security Council.

Although Özal's primary concern is the country's economic health, he has signaled his desire to allow Turkey to function as a bridge between NATO and the Middle East and has suggested that Ankara might play a larger role in the Arab world as well. He has, for example, offered Turkey's services in mediating an end to the Iran-Iraq War.[49]

Defense Cooperation

In March 1980 the United States and Turkey signed a Defense and Economic Cooperation Agreement (DECA) by which the United States committed itself to provide economic and defense support and to strengthen Turkish industrial capabilities. In return, the United States was given access to base facilities on Turkish soil. A joint U.S.-Turkish Defense Support Commission was established to ensure the most efficient utilization of U.S. funds. This was designed to complement the already existing Joint United States Military Mission for Aid to Turkey. The agreement solidified the U.S. defense cooperation effort, although the level of effort associated with the DECA has been criticized by some. A 1982 General Accounting Office study of the DECA concluded that there has been insufficient economic participation by other NATO members in the effort and that the sales terms were not favorable enough to allow Turkey to take full advantage of the program.[50] (A new DECA is being negotiated as this book goes to press.)

Efforts at assisting the slow pace of Turkish military modernization have increased during the Reagan administration. These efforts include a program to modernize airfields in eastern Turkey, suggesting a more overt role for Turkey in any Persian Gulf contingency. Although then–defense minister Bayulken denied that any specific role had been agreed upon that would associate Turkey with the RDJTF, he cautiously announced that "with its strong armed forces, Turkey as a member of NATO, will continue to be an element of equilibrium in the Middle East."[51]

The issue of Turkish participation in Persian Gulf contingencies has been a very sensitive one for *all* Turkish governments. Bayulken's statement resulted in further private details from Ankara, and during a visit to Turkey by U.S. Assistant Secretary of Defense Richard Perle in November 1982 (which was arranged for the signing of a bilateral memorandum on the modernization and use of airfields in eastern Turkey) the newspaper *Milliyet* reported that then–foreign minister Ilter Turkmen stated that while Turkey was not committed to an RDJTF mission, "when the need arises, the RDF [Rapid Deployment Force] could use not only the new bases but the old ones as well."[52] The statement referred to the U.S. desire to utilize these airfields in a Persian Gulf contingency, since the RDJTF would require staging areas and access to bases in order to reach the Persian Gulf. Despite such supportive public statements, the actual availability of these bases in a crisis is open to substantial question. If the United States was unable to use these facilities, Washington would be forced to look elsewhere, perhaps to Israel, for access.

Washington is also assisting in the modernization of Turkey's antiquated air-defense system. Older F–100s and F–104s will be replaced by F–16s. In addition, a number of F–4Es will be transferred to Turkey, and the Turkish government has asked for British Rapier SAM systems. As Turkey's ambassador to Washington, Súkru Elekdag, has noted, "The Turkish government's commitment to support the modernization of the Turkish Air Force reflects a new perception of the United States administration regarding the critically important roles played by Turkey within NATO."[53]

A major constraint on U.S. efforts to provide Turkey with economic and military assistance is the very effective lobbying effort of Greek-Americans. Although a number of factors have acted to limit U.S. assistance to Turkey, the Greek lobby has been able to galvanize support among a large number of U.S. legislators to punish the Turkish government for past policies, which were often seen as either anti-Greek or anti-Western. The influence wielded by the Greek lobby, however, is only one part of the problem. Unless Turkey is willing to accept a *firm* public commitment to support common Western security interests—including Soviet threats to the Persian Gulf—support from Congress will be mixed.

6.
GREEK-TURKISH FRICTIONS_____

The Aegean Command Dispute
and U.S. Base Rights

The Aegean dispute between Greece and Turkey includes several complex issues: delineation of the continental shelf, control of the sea, the vital airspace between the Greek and Turkish mainlands, and military jurisdiction. This discussion will be limited to the last two issues and how they have affected another difficult problem—NATO's inability to conduct military exercises in the Aegean.

Before Greece withdrew its military forces from NATO in 1974 in response to the Turkish invasion of Cyprus, Aegean defense was under the sole command of a U.S. officer based in Izmir, Turkey—the commander of the Sixth Allied Tactical Air Force (COMSIXATAF)—who had three subordinates, two Turkish officers and a Greek officer. The Greek commander had operational control of the airspace from the western coast of Greece to the Flight Information Region (FIR) boundary line off the west coast of Turkey. Thus, prior to 1974 the Greeks controlled air defense over most of the Aegean.[54] In addition, before 1964 the NATO command demarcation line was not the FIR line but rather a line roughly along 26° east longitude. Turkey never fully agreed to the change made by SACEUR in 1964, which made the air-defense line coincident with the FIR line.

To further complicate the situation, shortly after the 1974 Greek withdrawal Turkey ordered all eastbound planes to begin reporting to Turkish air-control authorities while they were still in Greek airspace halfway across the Aegean. The intention was to guarantee against the possibility of lightning strikes by the Greek air force.[55] Another development since the Greek withdrawal—the July 1978 action placing

COMSIXATAF under a Turkish rather than a U.S. commander—has further impeded a return to the pre-1974 command structure.

The dispute has been further inflamed by Greek rearmament of some of the Aegean islands in violation (the Turks argue) of both the 1923 Treaty of Lausanne and the 1947 Treaty of Paris, which established demilitarization of the islands. The Greek government has generally claimed that the rearmament decision was made necessary by the creation of the Turkish Fourth Army, deployed within striking distance of the Greek islands and essentially created to protect against Greek aggression. It should be pointed out, however, that the Greeks militarized the islands in 1964, eleven years before the creation of the Fourth Army.[56]

A NATO committee was established to resolve these very difficult issues—issues that, in the final analysis, involve important questions of sovereignty. General Alexander Haig, then SACEUR, took a very personal interest in this dispute, in part because of his feeling that the southern flank was a vital region in NATO and that should a crisis occur there, command and control would become issues of paramount importance. After consultations with General John Davos, the Greek representative, General Haig suggested in May 1978 that a new Greek command be established at Larissa, Greece, which would take operational control on an interim basis over the air defense of the entire Aegean up to the FIR line. The new commander in Larissa would be a Greek officer.

The Haig-Davos arrangement would have established a command structure for the Aegean similar to the pre-1974 arrangement except that a Greek commander would not be located at the same headquarters. Turkey disapproved of the proposal, arguing that once Greece reentered NATO, the interim proposal would become permanent because Greece (under NATO's consent rule) would be able to exercise an effective veto over any change. In October 1978 Turkey vetoed the first Haig approach. Haig offered two other approaches, neither of which was acceptable to both parties.

General Bernard Rogers, Haig's successor as SACEUR, has attempted to resolve the problem on several occasions but to date has not met with success. This dispute has now resulted in the disruption of NATO maneuvers on the southern flank. In 1983 NATO decided to exclude the Greek island of Limnos from its maneuvers because of Turkish protests over its militarization.[57] In September 1983 Greece withdrew from NATO naval maneuvers in the eastern Mediterranean after NATO's decision to exclude Limnos, which Athens read as U.S. acceptance of the Turkish position.[58] Athens also refused to allow a U.S. warship (destined for the U.S. Marines in Beirut) to load ammunition at the Souda Bay naval installation on Crete. This took place at a time when Syrian ships reportedly were being allowed to use Greek ports to resupply their troops in Lebanon.[59] In early 1986 Greece announced that it would participate in the next NATO exercise, despite a continuing dispute over Limnos.

Limnos lies just off the Turkish coast in the northeastern Aegean. Prime Minister Papandreou felt that agreeing to the exclusion would support the Turkish support on militarization. In November 1982 Papandreou had refused to allow Greek forces to participate in NATO maneuvers for the same reason, stating

> Limnos belongs to Greek territory and according to the Montreux Treaty, the Greek Government has every legal right to militarize it. Therefore, failure to recognize this right of the Greek Government within the framework of a NATO exercise is unacceptable to us.[60]

The Greek government has stated that the 1980 agreement, which brought Greece back into the NATO military structure, promised to restore all rights to which the Greeks had been entitled prior to their withdrawal. Others, including General Rogers, have taken a different interpretation of the 1980 agreement, holding that the agreement restored Greece's place within the Alliance, and provided for subsequent settlement of command and operational disputes.[61] A review of the public record suggests that General Rogers's interpretation is the valid one. Until the Aegean military issues are resolved, Greece's contribution to the region's defense will not be fully realized.

A Turkish Republic on Cyprus

In November 1983 the leader of the Turkish community on Cyprus, Rauf Denktash, declared that the northern portion of the island would thenceforth be the sovereign Turkish Republic of Northern Cyprus. Although northern Cyprus has been effectively split from the Greek Cypriot section of the island since Turkish forces invaded Cyprus in 1974, Denktash's declaration rejected the status quo of a federation on the island.

Turkish forces invaded Cyprus to reverse a coup attempt against the Greek Orthodox church leader and Cypriot president Archbishop Makarios. At that time Britain refused a Turkish request to support the invasion. Although the Turkish Cypriot leader had threatened to declare a sovereign state in the past, the move was not anticipated at that time. Private discussions held by the author with Turkish officials during visits to Turkey (1983, 1986) confirmed that the Turkish government (particularly the Foreign Ministry) was angered by the timing of Denktash's declaration, which came shortly before the December 1983 Turkish general elections.

Since February 1975 the Turkish Federated State of Cyprus has been the Turkish minority community of 150,000 on the island, founded with its own constitution and governing legislature. The Greek Cypriot community of 500,000 residents is led by President Spyros Kyprianou, who established his own federated state. The Turkish federated state was considered to be a component of the Greek-Turkish federation on Cyprus.

The November 1983 Denktash declaration was immediately condemned by the United States and by a UN Security Council resolution. Only Turkey has recognized the new state. As coguarantor of the 1960 treaty that gave Cyprus its independence, Great Britain announced that it would seek a reversal of the decision as part of a larger effort to achieve a settlement of the historical dispute. Questions were raised as to whether Britain had an obligation under the 1960 treaty to use military force to return the Turkish section of the island to its previous status. Britain maintains a small force of about 4,800 military personnel on the island, about 500 of whom are members of a 2,500-man UN force. They are stationed on two British military bases on the island.[62]

The Greek government quickly condemned the formation of a sovereign Turkish state on Cyprus, declaring that the Turkish government bore full responsibility for the action of the Turkish Cypriot leadership. The Turkish government has made clear its intention to support the new state including the use, if necessary, of the 18,000-man Turkish garrison on the island.[63] With the December decision by Denktash to form a national assembly on Cyprus, the opportunities for a settlement appear to be slim. The decision in April 1984 for Ankara to exchange ambassadors with northern Cyprus seemed to harden (for the time being) the November 1983 action.[64]

In January 1985, however, the leaders of the Greek and Turkish Cypriot communities agreed to meet for the first time in more than five years under the auspices of UN Secretary General Javier Pérez de Cuéllar at the UN in New York. Although a draft agreement received tentative approval by both sides prior to the UN talks, the meetings ended in failure over a number of issues, including the insistence of Denktash that Turkey remain a permanent guarantor of the Turkish Cypriot community's security.[65]

A number of individuals close to the UN talks, however, have suggested to the author that in discussions prior to the UN meeting, Kyprianou misled the UN secretary general into thinking the draft agreement presented no problems for him. As a result, Denktash arrived in New York under the false impression that an agreement was likely.

In March 1986 the UN secretary general submitted a new Cyprus proposal designed to break the deadlock. As this book goes to press, however, this latest proposal has not met with enthusiastic support from the Greek Cypriots, who have asked for major revisions to the document.[66] In addition, the Greek Cypriots have called for an international conference to discuss the Cyprus issue.

The Turkish Cypriots have accepted the UN plan. At this point the major issues separating the two sides are the continued presence of Turkish troops on the island, whether the northern portion of the island would retain any independence under the UN plan to reunify the island, and the question of the "three freedoms"—the right of all Cypriots to movement, settlement, and property in either zone. Kyprianou's suggestion for a conference comes three months after the Soviet Union proposed an international conference to discuss the need to demilitarize Cyprus.

The similarity of the Greek Cypriot proposal for an international conference and the earlier Soviet proposal reinforces the suspicion of many that Kyprianou regards Moscow as an ally in his continuing effort to reject any "solution" to the Cyprus dispute that strengthens the position of the Turkish Cypriot community. In addition, Kyprianou's support for the Soviet call to "demilitarize" the island reflects Soviet and Greek Cypriot concern that the Turkish Cypriots—in an effort to project a pro-Western stance—might boldly offer to establish a NATO base on the northern portion of the island.

7.

PAPANDREOU AND GREEK PARTICIPATION IN NATO

In October 1981 Andreas Papandreou, leader of the Panhellenic Socialist movement (PASOK) was elected prime minister of Greece in an impressive victory ending more than three decades of nearly uninterrupted conservative government. More important, the PASOK campaign platform called for radical changes in Greek foreign policy, particularly Greece's continued membership in NATO. Papandreou is bitterly anti-American, due in part to his belief that the United States engineered the April 1967 military coup in Greece that led to his imprisonment and exile.

Papandreou is as suspicious of NATO as he is of the United States. He does not believe that the Alliance (as it is presently configured) will be appropriately sensitive to Greek foreign and domestic interests. He also is much less concerned about the Soviet threat than he is about Turkish aggression directed toward Greece. In fact, Papandreou has adopted a cordial relationship with the Soviet Union. In February 1983 he issued a joint communiqué with then–Soviet premier Nikolai Tikhonov supporting the concept of a Balkan nuclear-free zone, which would mean removal of all U.S. nuclear weapons from Greek soil. He also supported the Soviet proposal for a Warsaw Pact–NATO nonaggression pact, which Alliance leaders have rejected categorically.[67] During the visit by Tikhonov, Papandreou signed a ten-year accord of economic cooperation that includes an agreement for the construction of a plant to mine 600,000 tons of alumina, which the Soviet Union requires for the production of aluminum metal.[68] Bilateral trade was to be increased from $570 million annually to $1.4 billion.[69]

In early February 1983 the U.S. administration announced that it would ask the Congress to appropriate $759 million in military assistance for Turkey in FY 1984, a dramatic increase from the previous year's appropriation of $402.7 million. The administration's aid request for Greece was $281.7 million, representing a modest increase of only $500,000 over the FY 1983 appropriation. In addition, President Reagan requested $175 million in economic support funds to promote the economic "stability" of Turkey, but requested no such funds for Greece.[70] Papandreou's reaction to the increase for Turkey was to threaten the suspension of bilateral talks with the United States on continued access to military bases on Greek soil. He also insisted on preservation of the 7:10 ratio in military aid to Greece and Turkey, respectively. In an interview after the U.S. aid request was announced, Papandreou stated that the U.S. bases in Greece "do not strengthen the country's national security and defense potential, nor are they related to our NATO obligations."[71]

Many have criticized the congressional maintenance of the 7:10 aid ratio, which for some time has served as the formula for determining U.S. military aid levels to Greece and Turkey. The principal objections to the ratio are that it (1) codifies Greek insistence that without such an arrangement Greece would be more vulnerable to Turkish aggression, and (2) implies that both states are of near equal strategic value to the United States and NATO. Clearly, Turkey is of greater value to NATO by virtue of its strategic position and its generally pro-Western policies. This state of affairs should be sufficient for the Congress to reject the ratio. In addition, Greek claims that Turkey wishes to conquer the Aegean islands are without foundation. As Robert W. Komer, former U.S. undersecretary of defense for policy (and a former U.S. ambassador to Turkey) has written, "Turkey needs Greece's nearby Aegean islands like it needs a hole in the head."[72] Ambassador Komer also called for congressional abandonment of the 7:10 aid ratio after the FY 1984 authorization was adopted.[73] The FY 1986 Reagan administration security assistance request to the Congress called for $785 million in assistance for Turkey and $500 million for Greece. The FY 1987 administration request represented a substantial increase for Turkey—to $900 million in military assistance and an additional $150 in economic support funds. The Greek aid level remained unchanged from the FY 1986 budget.[74]

The continued operation of U.S. bases is the major issue between the United States and Greece. Negotiations were suspended before the October 1981 Greek national elections and were finally concluded along with a Defense and Economic Cooperation Agreement in December 1983. During the course of the negotiations U.S. base negotiator Reginald Bartholomew had been told by Athens that the following four major issues had to be resolved before any agreement could be contemplated by the Greek government:

- Maintenance of the 7:10 ratio of U.S. military assistance to Greece and Turkey, respectively;
- A U.S. guarantee for the security of Greece's eastern boundary;
- Greek control over much of the activity on the U.S. bases; and,
- Additional sales of sophisticated weaponry previously denied to Greece.

The four bases in Greece are of critical importance to both the United States and to NATO. They include a deep-water port at Souda Bay, which is utilized by the U.S. Sixth Fleet, and air bases on Crete, which are central to NATO's defense of Greece and Turkey in the event of a Warsaw Pact attack. Although Papandreou seemed to have widespread popular support for closure of the U.S. facilities, the Greek military is probably less supportive. Papandreou has so far been able to retain the military's support, primarily due to his deep suspicion of Turkish foreign policy and his publicly stated view that a strengthened Greek military is the optimal deterrent to Turkish expansionism.[75]

The Reagan administration became alarmed at Greek behavior during the base negotiations as well as Papandreou's recent overtures toward Moscow. In a formal protest, former U.S. assistant secretary of state for European and Canadian affairs Richard Burt protested the Greek government's support for the Soviet-proposed Warsaw Pact–NATO non-aggression pact and Balkan nuclear-free zone concept.[76]

U.S.-Greek tensions rose as a result of the base negotiations and Papandreou's generally hostile attitude toward the Reagan administration. For example, the Greek government has protested emergency landings of U.S. aircraft at Souda Air Base in Crete. Summoned to explain the landings to Greek Deputy Minister of Foreign Affairs Ioannis Kapsis, then–U.S. ambassador Monteagle Sterns described them as emergencies, brought on by fuel problems and equipment failure.[77] The Greek government refused to accept his explanation.

The Greek government has also been hypersensitive to the movement of Turkish warships in the Aegean. During Aegean naval maneuvers in March 1984 a Turkish ship fired a number of shells, which the Athens government determined were directed at Greek ships in the vicinity of the maneuvers. After Papandreou announced that the incident was "the worst provocation against Greece since the 1974 Turkish invasion of Cyprus," he threatened to recall the Greek ambassador from Ankara and institute a military alert. Subsequently, the Greek foreign minister announced that "clarifications by Turkey" had resulted in a reversal of the Greek responses.[78]

Although the United States and Greece finally reached agreement on U.S. access to bases in Greece in 1984, Papandreou has since announced that when the current five-year agreement expires in 1989, the lease will not be renewed. This has resulted in a delay by Defense Department officials in implementing a $150 million construction program for the bases.[79] The delay is likely to continue until a renewal of the Greek DECA is negotiated in 1988. Pentagon officials have begun to plan for the transfer of certain Greek base facilities to either Turkey or Italy should Papandreou ask the United States to vacate them.

8.
SPANISH ENTRY
INTO THE ALLIANCE

Spain's formal admission to the NATO Alliance as its sixteenth member in May 1982 was greeted with great optimism by those who see a potentially critical role for Spain in NATO's security structure. A segment of the Spanish population has long viewed NATO membership as a prerequisite for acceptance as a modern, democratic European nation. More important for the Alliance, the Spanish military leadership has sought for some time to give its armed services a more projected role. Under Francisco Franco the Spanish military's only role was to protect the internal integrity of the Spanish state.

Spanish Debate on a NATO Role

It is not yet clear what role the Spanish will be willing to accept. Modernization of the Spanish armed services would require substantial investment by the Spanish if their defense role within the Alliance is to be significant. In addition, the Spanish military will have to be persuaded to cooperate more closely in planning, training, and exercises with their new allies—especially with the Portuguese, who have made no secret of their displeasure at having to share an Iberian command with Spain should the Spanish eventually integrate their forces.

Political changes within Spain could also affect the role of the Spanish military. The socialist election victory in Spain casts great doubt on Madrid's immediate contribution to NATO. A public referendum on Spain's continued membership in the Alliance was promised by the new regime, although the government of Felipe Gonzalez has shown considerably less enthusiasm than the Greek regime for a withdrawal from

NATO. In addition, the very poor showing of Spain's Communist party in the October 1982 elections has erased (temporarily perhaps) the possibility for any organized attempt by the Communists in parliament to gather support for a withdrawal decision. The number of Communist seats in the Spanish legislature dwindled to four and the long-time leader of its party, Santiago Carrillo, resigned in disgrace.[80]

On March 12, 1986, the Spanish people voted to remain in NATO, by a margin of nearly 13 percentage points.[81] The size of the victory was surprising, as many opinion polls had suggested a close vote and some even indicated majority support for a withdrawal decision. Although many greeted Spain's decision as a victory for the Alliance, a closer examination reveals the victory to be pyrrhic.

The Gonzalez government insisted on including three conditions with the referendum question. Spain would be prepared to remain in NATO only if: (1) Spanish forces would *not* be integrated into the NATO command structure; (2) Spain's status as a nonnuclear nation would continue; and (3) there would be a "progressive reduction of the U.S. military presence in Spain." The first condition essentially removes any Spanish military contribution to the Alliance. Gonzalez evidently determined that the Spanish public would reject continued NATO membership without these three conditions.

While it is important to note the unusual internal political conditions that formed the NATO debate in Spain,[82] it is more critical to recognize that this referendum may have created a dangerous precedent, encouraging other NATO states (notably Greece) to seek a similar arrangement whereby they may enjoy the guarantee of NATO's protective umbrella without contributing to its cost.

Portugal, the Iberian Peninsula, and the IBERLANT Issue

Spain's entry into NATO must be analyzed against the backdrop of its position on the Iberian Peninsula and the security contributions it would make as part of the Iberian Atlantic Command (IBERLANT) structure in which the Portuguese currently play the key role.

The triangle formed by continental Portugal, Madeira, and the Azores forms a strategic maritime and aerial zone potentially vital to southern flank security. It is an important support base for aerial resupply from the United States to the whole of Europe, North Africa, and the Middle East. In a limited conflict situation the triangle would be key to support air and sea communications, as was demonstrated in the Yom Kippur war. (At that time Portugal was the only NATO country that allowed the United States to use its facilities to transit supplies to Israel.) Also, the Azores would be the only mid-ocean base from which to conduct ASW operations in the Atlantic in time of war.

Although Portugal's potential strategic role is obvious, it is limited by a history of wrenching internal political upheaval. Its recent history has been anything but stable. Since the April 1974 coup d'état that ended nearly fifty years of dictatorship (under Antonio Salazar and his successor Marcello Caetano), Portugal has struggled for political stability. The most difficult period occurred between the 1974 coup and the restoration of democracy in 1976, during which time a succession of six provisional governments reigned. A similar series of political crises plagued Portugal in earlier attempts to forge a democratic coalition during sixteen years of democracy from 1910 to 1926; eighteen provisional governments ruled until a coup installed a military government.

There have been fifteen governments in Portugal since the April 1974 coup that brought a leftist Portuguese army colonel, Vasco Gonclaves, to power as prime minister. The Portuguese army had now come full circle, having installed a right-wing military figure in 1926. This was reversed, however, in 1975 in the first national elections to be held since 1926 in which the voters rejected continued military rule, choosing instead to support more moderate democratic parties including the Socialist party led by Mário Soares. Nearly eleven years after the April coup, Soares led the country as prime minister and in February 1986 was elected as the country's first civilian president in sixty years.

Although the Portuguese armed forces continue to wield some political power, the military commands only a fraction of its former influence. The reduction in the army's profile is due primarily to the decision to reduce drastically the size of the armed forces from a high of 210,000 to its current level of 73,000.[83] The army remains suspicious of the political leadership, due in part to the 1975 decision to grant independence to Portugal's African colonies.

The current leadership emphasizes Portugal's potential contribution to NATO both rhetorically and with a number of concrete actions, including a recent decision to form an air mobile brigade for the central front. In addition, Portugal continues to participate in joint NATO maneuvers, and the country plans to reinforce its navy by procuring several medium-size Dutch frigates. Further, the Portuguese continue to assure U.S. officials of the availability of the air base at Lajes in the Azores and the use of an underwater ASW listening station to monitor Soviet submarine traffic in the North Atlantic.

Portugal is struggling with serious internal difficulties (including a rising terrorist threat) and is striving to present its credentials as a modern European state (aided by its January 1986 entry into the EEC), deserving of a central place in the European security equation.

Furthermore, there are large questions concerning the command relationship between Spain and Portugal, although the Spanish government's current refusal to integrate its forces into the NATO command structure reduces the question to an academic exercise. Should a future Spanish administration reverse the Gonzalez nonintegration pledge, a Portuguese-Spanish military rivalry could erupt. Currently, Portugal discharges its NATO responsibilities through IBERLANT, which is a subordinate command of the Supreme Allied Commander, Atlantic (SACLANT). IBERLANT, headquartered in Lisbon, is responsible for the surveillance and control of 600,000 square miles of ocean from the Portuguese coast westward to 20° west longitude.

Lisbon has informed the NATO allies that it would never accept a Spanish commander for IBERLANT, although the Portuguese must recognize that some of Spain's vital interests do lie within the IBERLANT command area. The Portuguese would prefer that the Spanish focus their efforts in the Mediterranean. This is unlikely to happen, however, considering Spain's current naval and air operations in the Bay of Biscay and the Atlantic. Spain may expect to play a key role in IBERLANT and in the future, under a more conservative government than reigns today, may regard such a role as a necessary recognition of its status as a member of NATO. As noted earlier, however, Portugal is unlikely to cede its current command responsibilities willingly to the Spanish. Although the level of hostility between the two states does not approach that between the Greeks and Turks, the Iberian command situation is another example of how regional struggles between southern flank states tend to shift the focus inward, greatly impeding efforts to strengthen the region against the external Soviet threat.

Spain and the Iberian Peninsula

The Iberian Peninsula, because of its distance from central Europe and its accessibility from the Atlantic, would provide a secure rear area for logistic support of the central front in wartime and an ideal reception point for reinforcements from the United States. NATO forces could stage from Spanish air and naval bases and retreat to those bases if the war in central Europe went badly. Forces based in Spain would be in a strong position to dominate the western Mediterranean and the approaches to the Strait of Gibraltar, and Spanish holdings in the Baleares and the Canary Islands would further extend the Alliance's assets near the European theater. Spain's potential military contribution to NATO is not insignificant (as outlined in Table 9).

Access to Spanish bases could assume special importance for U.S. plans to move military forces perhaps through the U.S. Central Command

TABLE 9
Spanish and Portuguese Combat Forces (Selected Indicators) (1985–1986)

SPAIN	PORTUGAL
Army 1 armored division (1 armored, 1 mechanized brigade) 1 mechanized division (1 mechanized, 2 motorized brigades) 1 motorized division (2 motorized brigades) 1 armed cavalry brigade 1 parachute brigade (3 battalions)	1 mixed brigade 2 cavalry regiments 1 armored regiment 11 infantry regiments (3 independent infantry battalions)
Tanks: 319 AMX–30 350 M–47E 110 M–48	Tanks: 66 M–48A5
SAM: 10 Nike Hercules 24 Improved Hawk	SAM: 16 Blowpipe
Navy 7 submarines 1 carrier 11 destroyers 11 frigates 4 corvettes 12 fast-attack craft	3 submarines 17 frigates 19 patrol craft
Air Force 6 fighter squadrons (F–4C, Mirage) 2 fighter ground-attack squadrons[a] (F–5A, F–5B) 5 transport squadrons (C–130, KC–130)	4 fighter ground-attack squadrons 1 reconnaissance squadron 2 transport squadrons

Source: Data from *The Military Balance, 1984–1985, 1985–1986* (London: International Institute for Strategic Studies, 1984, 1985).

Note: This table presents a profile of military capability listing only those weapons and systems that the author regards as key indicators of military power.

[a]Spain will receive 72 F–18s. The first delivery of 9 aircraft was made in May 1986.

(CENTCOM) to the Persian Gulf. Madrid will understandably remain reluctant to make its facilities available for operations that relate in any way to the Arab-Israeli conflict, but as a NATO member it may be more forthcoming if allied leaders are able to argue convincingly that use of Spanish facilities for out-of-area contingencies serves Alliance *and* Spanish interests.

A potentially vital role for Spain would be its contribution to the ACE AMF. The AMF was intended to provide Alliance military forces capable of responding quickly to situations on the northern and southern flanks of NATO, where a single bordering nation on each flank—Norway in the north and Turkey in the south—has forces deployed. It is primarily a deterrent force—to involve the entire Alliance in resisting political-military pressures. Spanish bases and logistics facilities could significantly bolster the AMF's quick reaction capabilities.

Finally, the conditions for continued Spanish membership in NATO will in all probability pose problems for the Alliance. For example, Spain has entered NATO as a nonnuclear member, giving it a status similar to that of Denmark and Norway. Nuclear weapons may not be stored on Spanish soil. This raises potentially large problems if Spain is to be used as a forward operating area. In addition, U.S. overflight of Spain with nuclear-capable aircraft was a sensitive issue during negotiations with Madrid over U.S. base rights.[84] Despite the problematic character of the Spanish entry, however, the very presence of another solidly democratic southern flank state could provide incentive for NATO to begin to address seriously Spain's role in meeting security challenges to the region.

A number of issues have caused tensions between Madrid and Washington. The Gonzalez government announced that it would purchase 72 U.S.-built F–18 aircraft at a total cost of $2 billion. The contract was arranged during the 1982 base negotiations. Subsequently, Spanish Defense Minister Narcis Serra, after meeting with President Reagan, announced that the Spanish government was unhappy with U.S. efforts to reduce the trade imbalance between the two countries.[85]

In addition to the reluctance of the Spanish public to accept a military role in the Alliance, a number of internal issues affect Spanish thinking on NATO. Gibraltar is one of them. With its strategic location as the "Gateway to the Mediterranean," Gibraltar has been of vital concern to Great Britain. Although "the Rock" was formally ceded to Britain in 1713 under the Treaty of Utrecht, Spain has maintained its claim of sovereignty over the peninsula. The importance of Gibraltar to the strategic interests of NATO is its position guarding the Soviet naval exit from the Mediterranean. These concerns, along with a public referendum, which affirmed the desire of Gibraltar's population to remain

British, have prevented successive British governments from negotiating seriously with Madrid on the future of the fortress. During the Franco period the British were able to downplay Spanish demands to "return Gibraltar." With Spain's return to a democratic system these demands have become more difficult to ignore, as the successors to Franco are less willing to allow a permanent British presence there. Talks between the two governments on the Gibraltar issue continue with little progress.

Spain has threatened to withdraw from NATO if the Gibraltar issue is not resolved to its satisfaction. These threats were reiterated by journalists and Spanish legislators to the author during his 1984 trip to Spain. For a time many Spaniards regarded the return of Gibraltar as the quid pro quo for Spanish force integration, although (as mentioned earlier) the March 1986 referendum appeared to rule out integration of Spanish forces.

A number of solutions to the Gibraltar issue have been suggested. An interim solution, which would probably be satisfactory to all parties, would be a condominium arrangement between the British and the Spanish governments whereby the transition to Spanish rule would be gradual.

OPPORTUNITIES MISSED

As the preceding discussion has illustrated, NATO's southern flank presents a range of political, economic, and strategic difficulties unique within the Alliance's structure. A combination of "strategic bias" that favors central Europe at the expense of the flank regions and perpetuates the anemic political-military profile of the Mediterranean; interstate rivalries that severely limit opportunities to create a regional strategic partnership among NATO and Western-aligned states; and a sense shared by many Alliance leaders that "fringe" regions are by definition peripheral to NATO's security combine to dictate a very nearsighted perspective.

The Soviet Union is not unaware of this perspective. The Soviets may be encouraged to probe the limits of interventionism, if they conclude that the West's lack of concern over the deteriorating situation in the Mediterranean suggests that NATO would respond less forcefully to Soviet political and military pressure in that region than in central Europe. That conclusion would only be a logical extension of arguments made by a number of respected U.S. security analysts. In 1975, for example, a congressional research service study concluded, in a disturbing example of shortsighted analysis, that the loss of the southern flank would have no appreciable effect on the security of the central region.[86]

NATO's "central front bias" is not the only factor contributing to the West's lack of appreciation for the strategic value of the southern region. NATO strategy was adopted in an era of U.S. strategic superiority. It was believed that as long as the United States maintained a large margin of nuclear advantage over the Soviet Union, the East would be deterred from adventurism *anywhere* within the confines of NATO. Therefore, by this calculation NATO's flanks were as protected by the U.S. nuclear umbrella as was central Europe. By this same logic, however, if the credibility of the U.S. nuclear guarantee to central Europe erodes, so does the security of other areas within NATO Europe.

While the Alliance has modernized its nuclear delivery capability in the central region, it has allowed nuclear assets in the south to erode. At one time U.S. IRBMs in Italy and Turkey formed a critical component of the U.S. strategic retaliatory capability. As technological revolutions permitted the development of long-range intercontinental ballistic missiles (ICBMs), the strategic need for IRBMs disappeared. However, as the United States withdrew these antiquated systems from the southern region, it also removed a tangible symbol of the U.S. political guarantee to protect that territory with the same force as it protected other theaters in NATO Europe. The assumption that ICBMs based in the United States would replace the political component (as well as the strategic component) of the guarantee constituted a misreading of the importance with which both Turkey and Italy regarded the *presence* of these weapons. Clearly, there was no longer a strategic rationale for Jupiter and Thor deployments in the Mediterranean, but many in the region were surprised to find that Washington did not regard their replacement with newer systems as a pressing *political* priority. Indeed, NATO did not deploy a new generation of land-based nuclear weapons in Italy until 1983 as part of the NATO INF deployment. It is instructive to note the enthusiasm with which the Italian government and public greeted the deployment, as compared with the generally negative reaction that materialized in the other four NATO basing states, all of which are located in the central and northern theaters.

In Turkey the political damage of the Jupiter withdrawal has never been repaired. The author's discussions with current and former Defense Department officials suggest that Turkey was never seriously considered as a potential INF basing state. While it is far from clear that *any* Ankara government would welcome a new nuclear deployment, it is hard to imagine a more fractious or prolonged debate than that which occurred in the Netherlands, for example, where to this day it is unclear whether the 48 cruise missiles scheduled for deployment there in 1988 will in fact be deployed. The NATO council had an opportunity to offer cruise missiles to Turkey as a replacement for the Dutch deployment but chose not to do so.

Quite apart from the political opportunity that the Alliance missed in not considering Turkey in its original INF basing plan, NATO denied to itself what may have been a very effective military deterrent. The target set for ground-launched cruise missiles (GLCMs) based in Turkey would, presumably, include Soviet strategic air bases in the Transcaucasus from which Backfire bombers could be launched against much of NATO Europe. Cruise missiles in Turkey could therefore contribute to the Western deterrent far beyond its borders.

Clearly, one can debate the importance of NATO's refusal to address the deterioration of its nuclear posture in the south. Nevertheless, it does illustrate the narrow strategic and political prism through which the Alliance has evaluated both the contribution of southern flank forces to the overall NATO deterrent and the potentially negative effect *on all of* NATO of the erosion of regional power among the NATO nations on the southern fringe.

Part 2

U.S. AND ALLIED SECURITY POLICY IN THE PERSIAN GULF: OPTIONS AND DILEMMAS

The Persian Gulf Region

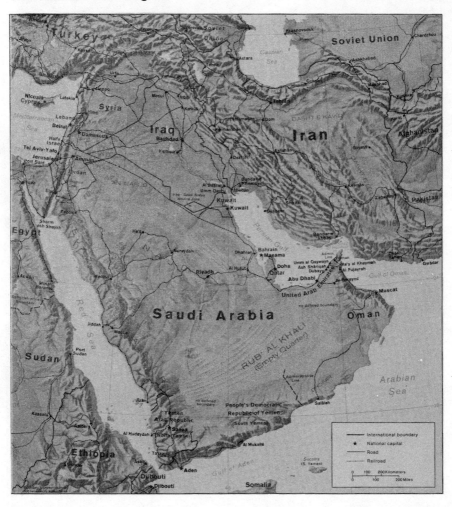

9.

AFTER AFGHANISTAN: A REASSESSMENT OF U.S. INTERESTS IN THE PERSIAN GULF

Defining U.S. interests in the Persian Gulf is difficult for those who have historically focused their attention and anxieties on the political-military balance in Europe, where the NATO and Warsaw Pact countries face each other with large military forces in a situation easily viewed as an East-West security dilemma. The Persian Gulf falls outside of the NATO formal treaty boundary; U.S. and Soviet troops do not face each other there. Nevertheless, Western interests are directly affected by developments in that region, and for that reason the gulf must figure prominently in U.S. security policy. One can quickly identify three factors that dictate the region's importance to the West: (1) the continuing (although reduced) Western dependence on Persian Gulf petroleum, (2) the region's vulnerability to military pressure from the Soviet Union, and (3) a long U.S. association with key states in the area.

For at least the foreseeable future, events in the Persian Gulf/ Southwest Asia (for the purposes of this paper, the "gulf" will be defined as including the region between Pakistan in the east and Egypt in the west) will seriously affect the economic health of the industrialized world. As Table 10 shows, while the percentage of dependency on Persian Gulf oil has been reduced in the United States, Europe, and Japan, the current flow of petroleum to Europe and Japan remains critical. The economies of Western Europe and Japan would be crippled if Persian Gulf oil supplies were denied for any significant period of time. The effect on the U.S. economy would be somewhat less dramatic, although not trivial.

TABLE 10
Persian Gulf Oil Dependency
(as % of total imports)

	1973 (Pre-Embargo)	1986[a]	% Decrease
UNITED STATES	13.2	7.3	44.7
WESTERN EUROPE	67.6	21.2	68.7
JAPAN	76.1	54.8	28.0

Source: International Energy Statistical Review, Central Intelligence Agency, 1986.
[a]Estimate based on first two quarters.

An Oil Crisis for the Producers

Recent dramatic shifts in the price of oil have threatened to reduce the economic and political power of OPEC. The thirteen-member cartel has seen a dramatic reduction in its ability to control the world market. Large discoveries of crude deposits in Alaska, Mexico, and the North Sea contributed to a reduction in OPEC's share of the oil market, from 63 percent of global output in 1979 to less than 38 percent in early 1986. In late 1985 and early 1986 the price of crude oil dropped by more than 60 percent to less than $10 per barrel. The drop reflected the reduced demand for crude, but the reduction in price was precipitated by a continuing struggle among OPEC members over production levels and price. The OPEC producers were unhappy with a self-imposed production ceiling of 16 million barrels per day. The ceiling was repeatedly violated, and by January 1986 total OPEC production was estimated at 18.5 million barrels per day.

Saudi Arabia was most responsible for the crisis, having doubled its daily production from 2 million to 5.5 million barrels. The Saudis hoped that by flooding the market, they might force other producers (within and outside of OPEC) to curb production, thus supporting the existing price structure and retaining as much of the profit margin as possible. A special committee of five OPEC members—Venezuela, Kuwait, Iraq, Indonesia, and the United Arab Emirates (UAE)—was appointed in December 1985 to determine OPEC's "fair share" of the declining market and to suggest ways to preserve it.

Saudi Oil Minister Sheikh Ahmed Zaki Yamani initiated an aggressive program to pressure other producers (particularly the British, whose North Sea oil competes with the light crudes of several OPEC producers) to lower their daily output. Other non-OPEC producers, such as Mexico and Norway, were also targets. The drop in world prices had already damaged the economies of even the more wealthy OPEC states. The plummetting of crude oil prices was the major contributor to a $12 billion budget deficit for the Saudis. Mexico was the most seriously threatened producer. With over 75 percent of its export revenues derived from oil production, Mexico might be unable to meet interest payments on a growing $96 billion foreign debt if the pricing crisis is not resolved.

A drop in oil prices, however, would be greeted with considerably more enthusiasm by the major consumers, particularly those among the Western industrialized nations. Chase Econometrics estimates that in the United States (which labored under a $145 billion trade deficit in 1985) for every drop in oil prices of $5 a barrel the trade deficit would be reduced by $9 billion. A truce in the OPEC price war has been reached, although it has become evident that the long-term implications of price instability could be grave for the West. Should the price of world oil remain below $15 a barrel, non–Middle East producers will soon find it uneconomical to continue pumping oil, while OPEC members (who are able to extract oil from the desert for .50 to .70 cents per barrel) will be able to continue production and possibly regain their earlier stranglehold on the world market. In short, lower prices for oil create large short-term gains for the West but potentially troublesome long-term consequences. Although OPEC's economic power has declined and reduced the prospects for a near-term supply or price crisis for the West, the superpower competition in the region endures and in many ways represents the last frontier of U.S.-Soviet rivalry.

A Shock to Détente

Since the gulf is quite obviously closer to the Soviet Union than to the United States, any potential Soviet military initiative in the region is of direct concern to the United States, inasmuch as U.S. allies there must depend on a U.S. security guarantee in the absence of an actual U.S. combat presence. With the Soviet invasion of Afghanistan in December 1979, a permanent "strategic shadow" was cast over the region. In an extremely efficient series of deployments, the Soviet Union moved thousands of troops and military matériel into Afghanistan, utilizing an elite corps of airborne divisions to secure the initial objectives. Although the Soviet occupation has proven more costly than Moscow planned, the initial invasion removed any doubt in the West about Soviet ability to mobilize quickly.

The most immediate effect of the invasion was to disabuse U.S. leadership of the illusion that a policy of détente was still in effect. President Carter's national security adviser, Zbigniew Brzezinski announced to a congressional hearing that the Soviet invasion should be viewed with great concern, that it represented "not a local but a strategic challenge."[87] This statement and others that followed suggested to some a fundamental alteration in the Carter administration's attitude toward the Soviet Union. This was confirmed in the president's January 23, 1980, State of the Union address, which has generally been labeled as the first utterance of a new "Carter Doctrine." The president declared that

> An attempt by an outside force to gain control of the Persian Gulf region will be regarded as an assault on the vital interests of the United States of America, and such an assault will be repelled by any means necessary, including military force.[88]

That such a statement was made so soon after the Soviet invasion suggests that this new "doctrine" was little more than empty rhetoric, devoid of analytical foundation. Clearly there had not been time for any serious reexamination of U.S. policy between the December 27 invasion and the January 23 address. Furthermore, it appeared that despite months of intelligence indications that the Soviets were mobilizing for an invasion, no serious contingency planning for a U.S. response was ever ordered. While a review of the memoirs of Brzezinski and of Carter's former secretary of state Cyrus Vance reveals that "contingency options" for a Soviet invasion of Afghanistan were requested, the president's lack of personal concern and appreciation for the strategic implications of a Soviet attack hobbled efforts of his advisers to respond to warnings that a crisis was imminent. For example, president Carter's response to Brzezinski's warning that the situation in Afghanistan was deteriorating was limited to ordering that "greater publicity be given to the growing Soviet involvement in southwest Asia."[89]

In contradictory elaborations of his new policy Carter freely admitted, on the one hand, that the United States had neither the intention nor the military capability to force a Soviet withdrawal from Afghanistan and, on the other, that his policy would ensure that the Soviet Union suffered "severe political consequences" for its actions.[90] The most immediate policy decision flowing from this view was the president's decision to request that the Senate defer its deliberations on ratification of the SALT II agreement, effectively killing the treaty. The deferment continues today. Other "sanctions" included trade restrictions, curtailment of Soviet fishing privileges in U.S. waters, suspension of an agreement to sell 17 million metric tons of grain to the Soviet Union, and U.S. withdrawal from participation in the 1980 Summer Olympic games in Moscow.

The United States was unable to obtain agreement from its European allies to condemn the Afghanistan invasion strongly and publicly or to take effective measures to restrict East-West trade as a reprisal. Secretary of state Vance failed in his attempts to sway the Europeans from an economic détente policy. In fact, West Germany actually increased its trade with the Soviet Union considerably in the wake of the invasion.[91]

The failure of the Carter administration to gather allied support for a hard-line, public Western position condemning the Soviet invasion of Afghanistan cannot be explained solely as a function of Western Europe's lack of resolve regarding perceptions of the Soviet threat. Clearly, there is a gap between U.S. and allied perspectives on the potency of Soviet military power, its application outside of Europe, and the range of appropriate Western responses to overt military incursions. Yet Europe's refusal to react to the invasion of Afghanistan with the same degree of alarm as evidenced by Washington was due largely to the cumulative effect of nearly three years of U.S. policy statements, which offered a relatively benign view of Soviet military power (particularly as applied in the Third World) and a generally apologetic atmosphere for Soviet violations of the mores of international behavior. This was reinforced by occasional statements by administration officials suggesting that Soviet foreign-policy objectives could be described as "defensive" and therefore not deliberately harmful to Western policy. Had the Carter administration announced a more assertive political-military policy toward Moscow in advance of the Afghanistan invasion and called for united Western opposition to Soviet incursions around the globe, Carter's pleas for Western support might have been received with greater sympathy.

The president's post-invasion declaration that the scales had been lifted from his eyes and that, henceforth, he could be relied upon to take a more sober and suspicious view of Moscow's behavior only confirmed to many West European leaders (particularly, for example, then–West German chancellor Helmut Schmidt) that the U.S. administration had miscalculated on a fundamental issue of East-West policy.

The Afghanistan invasion—and the continuing Soviet occuption of more than seven years—did have some salutary effect on Western strategy. It accelerated the process of Western debate over the "out-of-area" issue and laid the foundation for a more serious Western commitment to defending its interest in third areas. In that regard the announcement of the Carter Doctrine should be regarded as an important achievement. Nevertheless, the strategic effect of declarations made only *after* a crisis—rather than prior to them—is limited. The test will come if and when the Soviet Union chooses to probe the limits of the doctrine's application.

10.
FROM TRUMAN TO NIXON: REGIONAL DOCTRINES IN HISTORICAL PERSPECTIVE

The attempt by the Carter administration to formulate a new doctrine to guide its policy in the Persian Gulf/Middle East should be judged against both the history of U.S. deployments in the region and the events that provoked a reassessment of U.S. strategic interests there. U.S. policy toward the gulf region in the postwar era can be divided into five distinct periods: (1) the Truman Doctrine of 1947, (2) the formation of the Baghdad Pact (which evolved into the Central Treaty Organization (CENTO), (3) the Eisenhower Doctrine, (4) the Nixon Doctrine, and (5) the Carter Doctrine, the instruments of which endure today through the Central Command (CENTCOM), successor to the original Rapid Deployment Force (RDF) and the Rapid Deployment Joint Task Force (RDJTF). President Reagan's strategic policy toward the region, while more vigorous than Carter's, is not a distinct departure from it and thus does not constitute a new period. Although a "Reagan Doctrine" has been hailed by many observers (particularly in light of the April 1986 U.S. bombing of Libya), the Reagan administration's strategic concepts have had more of a global rather than a regional emphasis. The "Reagan Doctrine" has to date focused on administration support for insurgencies struggling to overthrow repressive regimes in Afghanistan, Nicaragua, and Angola. Reagan has not articulated a regional security strategy that focuses on the Persian Gulf/Middle East.

The Development of Soviet Interests

During the last four decades U.S. policy alternated between two prominent and linked strategic concerns—protecting the flow of oil to the West and deterring Soviet political-military ambitions in the region. There was at times an ironic connection between these two concerns. For example, as early as 1944 the Soviet Union, apprehensive about emerging U.S. and British interests in Iran, reminded Washington that Moscow possessed "proven rights to oil exploration in Iran."[92] In that same year the Soviet ambassador in Tehran assured the newly appointed U.S. ambassador to the Soviet Union, W. Averell Harriman, that Soviet interests extended beyond oil exploration to the internal political landscape and that while the Iranian people might be unsure as to their needs and desires, Moscow labored under no such uncertainty. He added that since Moscow "knew what the Iranian people wanted, it was proper for the Soviet government to see that this opinion found political expression."[93] This implicit threat created a linkage between U.S. concern for preserving the internal stability of Iran and deterring Soviet military intervention in the region. The concern provoked by Soviet interest in Iran soon created the conditions for superpower rivalry in the region. Over a period of time, the Iranian Communist party, Tudeh, began to assume a decidedly pro-Soviet tone. Soviet interests in Iran's internal disruptions extended through the 1979 revolution, which brought the Ayatollah Khomeini to power. At the height of civil unrest and strikes in Kurdistan in November 1978, Moscow warned Washington not to intervene.[94]

Since the close of World War II the United States and the Soviet Union have sought to frustrate or prevent each other from orchestrating or participating in regional alliance systems in the Middle East. The Soviets have often pressured key states into avoiding alliances that Moscow considered to be hostile to its regional interests. After the formation of the Baghdad Pact (whose initial membership included Iraq, Turkey, and Great Britain) in February 1955, the Soviet Union began to pressure Iran not to consider joining the Pact, reminding Tehran about its obligations under a 1927 Soviet-Iranian treaty that, in the Soviet interpretation, forbade either signatory from entering into "political alliances or agreements directed against" the other.[95] Iran ignored the Soviet warning and joined the Pact in 1955. Despite Soviet anger at Tehran's accession to a Western security instrument, Moscow continued to maintain friendly relations with Tehran.

The grand scheme of the Pact was to create a Western-oriented security system for the Middle East, but its exclusion of potentially key participants created interstate tensions. Pact members Iraq and Pakistan were Western-oriented, while Egypt and Afghanistan (whose policies were more sympathetic to Moscow) did not join and subsequently turned to the Soviet Union for arms support.[96]

The Eisenhower Doctrine

With the failure of the Suez expedition in 1956 and the growing disaffection of Egypt's president Gamal Abdel Nasser with the West (illustrated by his encouragement of the Soviet agreement to finance the Aswan Dam after the Western offer was withdrawn), president Eisenhower in 1957 formulated a policy of economic development for Middle Eastern nations to include military assistance and cooperation to those governments attempting to protect themselves against the forces of "international communism." In a special message on the Middle East before a joint session of Congress, Eisenhower proposed that the United States should grant

> such assistance and cooperation to include the employment of the armed forces of the United States to secure and protect the territorial integrity and political independence of such nations requesting such aid against overt armed aggression from any nation controlled by international communism.[97]

The Eisenhower Doctrine (formally adopted as Public Law 7 by the eighty-fifth Congress) is generally interpreted as an attempt to slow the evolution of Soviet influence in the Middle East. In his memoirs, the former editor of *Al Ahram* (and twice a cabinet member in the Nasser government), Mohammed Heikal, concluded that the deterrence of international communism was a pretext "behind which the U.S. sought to offer itself as the replacement for Britain and France as the dominating influence in the Middle East."[98] Where the United States expressed concern over Nasser's "neutralism," Arab statesmen applauded Nasser's support for Arab "nationalism." Reflecting Eisenhower's concern over creeping Soviet influence in the Middle East and secretary of state John Foster Dulles's publicly expressed intolerance of Arab neutralism in a region he believed crucial to the success of U.S. policy in the cold war, the scope of the Eisenhower Doctrine was broadened to include support for regimes under internal political attack. Congress appropriated $200 million in FY 1957 to finance the doctrine. The first application of U.S. funds under the Eisenhower Doctrine supported Jordan's King Hussein in his increasingly difficult battle with left-wing opposition groups in the Hashemite Kingdom.[99] In 1958, again under the Eisenhower Doctrine, U.S. Marines landed in Lebanon in an attempt to end a civil war there.

The comparison with the Reagan administration's involvement in Lebanon is inescapable. At the time of the U.S. landing in 1958 the U.S. Sixth Fleet was virtually unopposed in the eastern Mediterranean. The Soviet Fifth Escadra had not yet been formed, and at that time only a small portion of the Soviet Black Sea Fleet would have been available had the Soviet Union decided to oppose the U.S. intervention. Current Soviet deployments in the Mediterranean are considerable, and, except during temporary U.S. surge deployments (such as that of the U.S. battleship *New Jersey* and its escorts in 1984 or the 3-carrier task group deployed in March 1986 during the second Gulf of Sidra crisis) or major naval exercises, they are nearly equal to the U.S. naval presence in terms of surface combatants.

The 1967 Arab-Israeli War marked a historical threshold in U.S. policy toward the region. Washington's assistance to Israel during the war signaled a de facto U.S. alliance with the Jewish state that sharply divided the Arab world. An Arab "rejectionist" confederation led by Iraq and Syria slowly crystallized around two issues: (1) opposition to Israel's survival as a sovereign state, and (2) an increasingly anti-American Arab policy toward Israel's prime benefactor, the United States. Other more moderate states led by Egypt, Jordan, and Saudi Arabia emphasized the necessity for a U.S. role in any settlement of the Arab-Israeli dispute and, therefore, continued publicly to support Washington as a broker.

Britain's Withdrawal

As the U.S. diplomatic role in the Middle East increased, it became clear that Great Britain was seriously considering withdrawing from the region and terminating its security commitments in areas east of Suez. The 1956 Suez crisis confirmed Whitehall's fears that the British Empire would soon be forced—principally by budgetary priorities—to reduce severely its military commitments abroad. Leading historians and commentators began publicly to question Britain's ability to defend an overseas network of military bases and, therefore, the prudence of maintaining them. As early as 1950 the British historian B. H. Liddell Hart had concluded that the remnants of the empire were increasingly vulnerable and thus represented liabilities for Britain, rather than strategic assets.[100] In addition, the Middle East was no longer regarded to be as strategically vital to Great Britain as its commitments in the Far East. Shifting British troops and equipment from the Middle East would, for example, allow London to augment its presence in Hong Kong.[101]

Britain's withdrawal from the Mediterranean actually began before the Suez invasion. In 1950 British forces withdrew from Greece and, in 1955, from the Sudan. Between 1954 and 1956 the British also phased out their bases in Egypt, which until then were the focal point for British military power in the Middle East. Britain did retain a number of key facilities in the area, however, some of which were utilized in the aborted 1956 invasion of the Egyptian Canal Zone.[102]

The first serious government-mandated study of British commitments east of Suez was ordered by Conservative prime minister Harold Macmillan in 1958. That year the Baghdad Pact collapsed and was soon resurrected as the Central Treaty Organization (CENTO). The immediate result was a delay in British withdrawal, as Macmillan's committee determined that British possessions east of Suez had assumed greater strategic value for the empire.[103]

In the early 1960s Washington became concerned that a British withdrawal would create a political-military vacuum that only the United States could be expected to fill. As the U.S. commitment to the war in Southeast Asia increased, Washington shuddered at the prospect of having to replace the British east of Suez. As a result, the Johnson and Nixon administrations were both publicly and privately supportive of the British presence in the Middle East. There was, however, increasing domestic opposition in Great Britain to a British role in the region. The opposition Labour party, for example, called for the government to abandon "outmoded military bases abroad."[104] A consensus began to develop, and in January 1968 the Labour government of Harold Wilson announced that British forces would be withdrawn from the gulf (and the Middle East) by 1971.[105] When the Conservatives assumed power again, they did not reverse the previous government's decision to withdraw. One week before the withdrawal announcement, Aden (a key British possession and military base) was granted its independence. As Her Majesty's government had explained the necessity to withdraw British forces as a function of fiscal constraints, the four gulf sheikhdoms of Bahrain, Qatar, Abu Dhabi, and Dubai (the latter two of which are the principal emirates of the United Arab Emirates founded in 1971) offered to underwrite the continuance of a British military presence. According to British author David Watt, the oil shiekhdoms would be assuming an annual maintenance cost of £12 million.[106] The British declined the offer and withdrew, suggesting that revised British strategic concerns rather than fiscal constraints were the genuine reasons for the retreat.

The Nixon Doctrine

The Nixon administration came to office in January 1969, one year after the British withdrawal announcement. Although initial preoccupation with the Vietnam War prevented U.S. policymakers from looking beyond the immediate theater of concern—Asia—some were already drawing strategic lessons from U.S. involvement in Southeast Asia. In

October 1967, in an article published in *Foreign Affairs*, Richard Nixon hinted at a larger strategy, which would become the Nixon Doctrine. Nixon warned that the Vietnam conflict had "imposed severe strains on the United States" and that there were "serious questions whether the American public or the American Congress would now support a unilateral American intervention, even at the request of the host government." Asia provided the immediate context for Nixon's warning, but the implications for other vital regions were obvious. Nixon declared that two conditions would have to be met in the future if the United States was expected to respond to crises around the globe: (a) "a collective effort by the nations of the region to contain the threat by themselves," and if that effort failed, (b) "a collective request to the United States for assistance."[107]

The first of these two conditions was to become the basis for a regional security doctrine with direct application to the Middle East. The first suggestion of a Nixon Doctrine came during a press conference held by the president in 1969 on Guam, at the beginning of his trip to Asia. The president, in response to a question about the implications of a U.S. withdrawal from Vietnam, declared

> . . . as far as the problems of internal security are concerned . . . the United States is going to encourage and has a right to expect that the problem will be increasingly handled by, and the responsibility for it taken by, the Asian nations themselves.[108]

Since the formulation of the Nixon Doctrine, U.S. administrations have been concerned about a power vacuum but reticent about committing U.S. forces to the Persian Gulf/Middle East region. They have consistently sought to develop regional strategies that identify key allies or surrogates that might assume the burden of Western security with a U.S. military presence just "over the horizon." Although the context for the doctrine's formulation was the prolonged U.S. commitment to South Vietnam, the logic of Nixon's model also applied to the Middle East, where the two superpowers were becoming directly involved in the region's military security.

The key components of the Nixon Doctrine were developed in a televised address to the nation on November 3, 1969. Although he focused the speech on the war in Vietnam, Nixon was extrapolating from the Vietnam tragedy to construct a global U.S. policy. He declared (in a speech in which he became famous for his appeal to the "great silent majority of my fellow Americans") that a precipitous withdrawal from Vietnam would "spark silence wherever our commitments help maintain the peace—in the Middle East, in Berlin, eventually even in the Western Hemisphere."[109] He outlined three principles that would

> not only help end the war in Vietnam, but which is an essential element of our program to prevent future Vietnams:
>
> - First, the United States will keep all of its treaty commitments.
> - Second, we shall provide a shield if a nuclear power threatens the freedom of a nation allied with us or of a nation whose survival we consider vital to our security.
> - Third, in cases including other types of aggression, we shall furnish military and economic assistance when requested in accordance with our treaty commitments. *But we shall look to the nation directly threatened to assume the primary responsibility of providing the manpower for its defense.* (Emphasis added.)[110]

The Nixon Doctrine was formally introduced to the U.S. Congress on February 18, 1970, in what was billed as "the First Annual Report on United States Foreign Policy." The report, entitled *Foreign Policy of the 1970's: A New Strategy for Peace*, announced the central thesis of the Nixon Doctrine:

> The United States will participate in the defense and development of allies and friends, but America cannot—and will not—conceive *all* the plans, design *all* the programs, execute *all* the decisions and undertake *all* the defense of the free nations of the world.[111]

In the section of the report dealing with the Middle East Nixon reaffirmed his intention to "maintain a careful watch on the balance of military forces and to provide arms to friendly states as the need arises."[112] The Nixon Doctrine began to assume concrete dimensions as the administration articulated its strategy for regional security. A centerpiece of the doctrine (with direct application to the Middle East) was the president's September 15, 1970, message to Congress requesting reform of the foreign assistance program. In the report, entitled *Foreign Assistance for the Seventies*, Nixon directly linked increased assistance to the success of a regional security initiative.[113]

The doctrine, as applied to the Middle East, had three broad objectives:

1. To negotiate an Arab-Israeli settlement;
2. To reduce or remove entirely the Soviet influence and presence in the region;
3. To secure U.S. access to Persian Gulf petroleum, principally through the establishment of strong key regional allies—Iran and Saudi Arabia. This would require large programs of military and

economic assistance to develop viable military forces in these
two countries. Iran and Saudi Arabia were to become the "two
pillars" of U.S. policy in the region.

Implicitly, the United States would (according to the Nixon-Kissinger
calculus) be able to (1) fill the vacuum left by the British without actually
committing U.S. military forces to the region, and (2) protect against
the rise of a radical regime in the key oil-producing region of the Persian
Gulf by arming Iran and Saudi Arabia. It was hoped this would create
superpower surrogates that would act as the gulf states' protectors and
serve as a deterrent to Soviet intervention in the region. Although the
military assistance component of the Nixon Doctrine emphasized arms
transfers rather than a U.S. presence, the need for U.S. advisers became
greater than originally anticipated in both Iran and Saudi Arabia. By
1976, for example, there were roughly 25,000 "military-related" U.S.
personnel and dependents in Iran.[114]

The Nixon policy toward Iran and Saudi Arabia represented the
two parallel tracks of U.S. strategy in the gulf. Iran would act as the
military-strategic ally and Saudi Arabia, the economic-strategic partner.
Concern over the reliability of an uninterrupted flow of oil to the West
dictated Washington's policy toward Riyadh. Arms sales to the Saudis
were designed primarily to bolster the Faisal monarchy against internal
disruption rather than to create (as with Iran) a regional military surrogate.
Reinforcing the authority of the House of Saud would, according to the
Nixon-Kissinger strategy, hedge against the crystallization of anti-U.S.
sentiment within the royal family and the country itself. There was also
the hope that an arms transfer dependency on the United States might
temper Saudi oil pricing policy to the West.

Just as the Iranians began to chafe under U.S. pressure, so did the
Saudis, who became increasingly irritated with attempts by the United
States to balance its policy toward Riyadh against a continuing need to
reassure the Israeli government that the United States was not seeking
to create an Arab military counterweight against Israel's growing capability. Meanwhile the Saudi regime was not reticent about reminding
Washington that Moscow did not labor under such political pressures
and that, therefore, a Soviet security arrangement might be as attractive
to Riyadh as a partnership with the United States.

Although the U.S.-Iranian partnership was originally formed by a
convergence of events and the congruence of Nixon's view of Soviet
ambitions in the Middle East with the shah's desire to be the "policeman
of the gulf," a shift in Iran's overtly pro-Western oil-pricing policies
evolved in the aftermath of the 1973 Arab-Israeli War, placing the
relationship under great strain. This became particularly acute during

the 1973-74 Arab oil embargo. The shah pursued a pricing policy that at times created questions about whether he felt his obligation to OPEC predominated over his commitment to the United States. This led to a debate over whether in fact the large U.S. arms transfers to the shah ($11.9 billion from FY 1969 to FY 1976, or 24.3 percent of U.S. worldwide foreign military sales)[115] actually contributed to his decisions to raise the price of Iranian crude to the United States. Some draw a causal link between the ability of the gulf states to purchase arms and the necessity for increased oil revenues to finance such transactions,[116] while others are not persuaded that oil price increases were the result of expensive arms sales necessitating greater revenues.[117]

Regardless of how one interprets the cause for the strains in the U.S.-Iranian alliance, the shah remained confident that so long as Richard Nixon remained in the White House, his "special relationship" with the United States was safe, despite calls by the U.S. Congress to restrict future arms sales to the shah in light of his unfriendly oil-pricing policies. It is interesting to note that little concern was voiced on Capitol Hill over the shah's stability on the Peacock Throne despite early indications of internal challenges. President Nixon's policies toward Iran endured until president Carter's inauguration, although subsequently president Ford was less inclined to treat the shah in the royal manner to which he had become accustomed during the Nixon administration.

Clearly, president Nixon was struggling to create a realignment in the Middle East "to construct a completely new set of power relationships" there.[118] Although Nixon's arms transfer policy in the region focused on Iran and Saudi Arabia, a third country—Egypt—also figured in the Nixon-Kissinger strategy. The Egyptian relationship with Moscow had strong historic roots, but president Nixon initially felt that obstacle could be vaulted, particularly if the Soviet Union was included in any peace effort.

During the 1969-70 Arab-Israeli "war of attrition," president Nixon invited the Soviet Union to join a series of discussions designed to negotiate a solution to the West Bank dispute. This invitation was a tacit recognition by Washington that the Soviet Union had some responsibility for regional security issues. Unfortunately (and predictably) Soviet participation in these talks only exacerbated regional tensions and tended to reassure Egyptian president Nasser that Moscow would guarantee that Egypt's interests were considered in any settlement. The Moscow-Cairo understanding became obvious when president Nasser traveled to Moscow in January 1970 in search of a new Soviet arms transfer relationship. As a result of that trip the Soviet Union agreed to supply Egypt with MIG–21 aircraft and SAM–2 and SAM–3 missiles. In addition, Soviet pilots began to fly patrols in the Nile Valley.[119]

In the aftermath of the 1967 war the Egyptians signed a five-year agreement with Moscow, which provided the Soviet Union with naval access to Alexandria, Port Said, and Mersa Matrûh.[120] This strategic partnership continued until Soviet-Egyptian relations soured. President Nasser died in 1970, and the tone of Soviet-Egyptian relations changed dramatically, as Nasser's successor, Anwar Sadat, was markedly less enthusiastic about a long-term strategic arrangement with Moscow. In 1972 much of the Soviet naval access was curtailed when control of the shore installations returned to the Egyptians.[121] The military relationship ended in 1976 when president Sadat expelled all remaining Soviet advisers.

President Nixon soon realized that his invitation to the Soviet Union to become directly involved in the Middle East peace process created a new set of pressures in the region. As early as 1970 Henry Kissinger (then the president's national security adviser) declared that "the goal of American policy was to expel the Russians from the Middle East."[122] The Egyptian government, then under president Sadat's leadership, quickly realized the risks that attended an alliance with Moscow, as illustrated by Sadat's desperate overture to Washington at the conclusion of the 1973 Arab-Israeli War. Despite the massive U.S. airlift to Israel during the war, Sadat restored diplomatic relations with Washington after a hiatus of seven years.

The Nixon Doctrine, as applied to the Middle East, was at best a limited success. The "two-pillar" strategy ultimately failed in Iran, as internal upheaval brought not only a radical leadership change but also a political-cultural and social metamorphosis (with wider parameters than were envisaged by the most prescient regional specialists).[123] In addition, U.S. support for Saudi Arabia signaled Washington's willingness to reinforce a key oil producer whose ability to embrace publicly a Western-oriented security policy was severely limited. Although Nixon's attempts to include the Soviet Union in Middle East peace efforts failed, that failure illustrated Moscow's genuine agenda in that part of the globe—to contest any U.S. presence and influence in the region.

11.
THE REGIONAL SECURITY LANDSCAPE

In order to understand the complex interstate relationships that compose the Persian Gulf, it is necessary to describe the regional institutions and alliances around which political, economic, and security issues are formed.

The Gulf Cooperation Council

In May 1981 the heads of state of the six gulf nations—Saudi Arabia, Kuwait, Oman, Qatar, Bahrain, and the United Arab Emirates—meeting in Abu Dhabi, signed the charter of the Gulf Cooperation Council (GCC) and created the first Persian Gulf collective security system.[124] The principal policymaking body for the GCC is the Supreme Council, which is made up of the heads of state of the six member nations with a chairmanship rotating in alphabetical order. The council meets in regular session, twice yearly. There is also a Commission for the Settlement of Disputes to arbitrate issues between the members. The Ministerial Council—in practice, the key decisionmaking institution of the GCC, which rules on all key appointments to council posts—is comprised of the foreign ministers of the member states and meets six times a year. The General Secretariat assumes responsibility for the daily business of the council, which is conducted through an appointed secretary general.

The GCC was founded primarily to create a regional mechanism for interstate consultation on a wide range of economic and security issues affecting the six "conservative" gulf states. The emphasis initially was on facilitating joint investment in cooperative economic institutions, such as the Gulf Investment Corporation, founded in 1983. Each state was to contribute $350 million to this pool, creating one of the largest cooperative investment funds in the Middle East.[125]

The catalyzing event for the GCC's formation in February 1981 was the fall of the Iranian shah and the opening of hostilities between Iran and Iraq in September 1980. The security policy function of the council has evolved steadily from the initial decision to establish a National Security Council with vaguely defined responsibilities to a more serious effort to investigate the feasibility of defense cooperation among GCC members. In December 1982 a Defense Council was formed with a mandate to address seriously the problems of standardization and interoperability of military equipment among the members states, consideration of a unified gulf military command, maritime surveillance, and cooperative military training. Political timidity and the lack of any perceived, imminent military threat, however, hobbled initial efforts at implementation of these plans.

Pressure from the revolutionary regime in Tehran to scuttle the council's plans for genuine military cooperation was the prime reason for the lack of enthusiasm for greater integrative defense programming within the council. The Ayatollah Khomeini feared that the GCC could become supportive of Iraq's war effort against Iran. Yet even without the Iran-Iraq War casting a political shadow over the GCC's deliberations, the member states found it difficult to arrive at a consensus on questions of collective security.

There were multiple reasons. The GCC members do not share the same level of concern over security threats to the region, nor are they uniformly capable of defending against such threats. In addition, the ability of individual GCC nations to support large military expenditures also varies greatly. But most important, the GCC suffers from a lack of corporate leadership, in large part because the most powerful member— Saudi Arabia—has refused to assume a larger role as a security guarantor. In light of Saudi King Fahd's reticence the United States should reconsider whether its current level of foreign military sales and construction—$4 billion in the Reagan administration's FY 1987 request[126]—is compatible with both Saudi will and capability to perform a role as a regional ally. If not, a portion of these funds[127] might be more profitably invested in other states that have either exhibited more enthusiasm for such a role or that could be persuaded to accept it. Turkey and Oman are prime examples.

Historic rivalries among the members also contributed to the lack of progress. The UAE, for example, remained suspicious of Oman's growing military prowess and the potential influence of Oman's Sultan Qaboos over Omanis who served in the UAE armed forces. In addition, economic competition among the members began to sour interstate relations. As a world oil glut developed soon after the GCC's inauguration, the members began to compete with each other for reduced shares in a seriously declining world oil market. This created fissures between Saudi Arabia and the other five council members, as Riyadh insisted on OPEC pricing and production ceilings. Oil feuds between Saudi Arabia and Iran over export policy added to the political pressure applied to the smaller gulf states by the Khomeini regime.

However, as the Iran-Iraq War dragged on without any sign of a definitive conclusion, the GCC began to address more seriously the need for integrative security mechanisms and in 1984 established the framework for a gulf rapid deployment force, the "Peninsula Shield," to be comprised of 12,000 troops drawn from the six GCC members and placed under the command of a Saudi general.[128] Joint arms production was included in the planning for the shield. A regional air-defense network was also discussed in the wake of the much-publicized U.S. sale of AWACS to Saudi Arabia. The GCC members unanimously supported the sale; had Congress refused to approve it, GCC relations with Washington would have been adversely affected.[129]

Small, joint GCC military exercises were planned and carried out in 1983 and 1984. In addition, the Ministerial Council accelerated efforts for regional military planning following the decision by NATO defense and foreign ministers in the spring of 1983 not to extend formally NATO's defense umbrella to the gulf.[130] In 1984 GCC members became alarmed over the increasing frequency of attacks on gulf shipping by both Iran and Iraq, including attempts by Iraq's President Saddam Hussein to destroy Iran's principal oil terminal at Kharg Island. The air forces of Bahrain, Qatar, Saudi Arabia, and Kuwait began to hold joint maneuvers to exercise their meager air-defense forces.

Although council members have been cautious about overtly supporting either of the two belligerents in the Iran-Iraq War, a consensus emerged among the members in 1984–85 that further efforts to persuade Iran to limit its military reprisals against GCC members for their sporadic support of Iraq's war effort would be fruitless. The Iranian attacks have brought the Saudis closer to the other five GCC members and provoked strong statements uncharacteristically from the Saudi government, suggesting that Saudi Arabia might become involved in the Iran-Iraq War if Iran attempted to close the Strait of Hormuz, as Khomeini's lieutenants threatened. Saudi Defense Minister Prince Bandar bin Sultan was quoted as saying, "Saudi Arabia will defend freedom of navigation in the Gulf if Iran carries out its threats. It is Iran's right to talk and our right to defend."[131]

TABLE 11
GCC Military Balance (1985–1986)

	SAUDI ARABIA	KUWAIT	BAHRAIN
Population (millions)	8	1.8	.4
Gross National Product (GNP)ᵃ ($ billions)	110	29	4.1
Defense Expendituresᵃ (as % of GNP)	24.3	4.0	4.0
Total Military Manpower	62,500	12,000	2,800
Army (selected indicators)	3 armored brigades 3 mechanized brigades 1 infantry brigade 5 artillery battalions 14 SAM batteries Tanks: 300 AMX–30, 150 M–60 A–1	2 armored brigades 1 mechanized infantry brigade 1 SSM battalion Tanks: 70 Vickers Mk 1, 10 Centurion, 160 Chieftain	1 brigade: 1 infantry squadron, 1 armored car squadron, 1 artillery battery
Navy (selected indicators)	4 frigates 4 corvettes 1 patrol craft	8 fast-attack craft 48 patrol craft 3 amphibious vessels	4 fast-attack craft
Air Force (selected indicators)	3 squadrons fighter ground-attack aircraft (F–5E) 4 squadrons interceptors (F–53, T–55, F–15) 4 E–3A (AWACS) 24 helicopters	2 squadrons fighter ground-attack aircraft 1 squadron interceptors 3 squadrons helicopters	6 fighter ground-attack aircraft (F–5E, F–5F) 1 squadron helicopters

The Regional Military Balance

The political-military landscape of the Persian Gulf is a difficult one to comprehend, in part because conventional East-West labels are not entirely appropriate or accurate. That said, one is forced to use some method of classification in order to describe the regional military situation. For the purposes of this study the GCC members will be thought of as Western-aligned or "conservative," while the states of Iran, Iraq, and South Yemen will be regarded as hostile. Saudi Arabia is the clear leader of the Western-aligned states, while Iran is the dominant hostile state. Clearly, there are degrees of alignment and hostility in both groups. The state most difficult to classify is North Yemen, which, while not Marxist has rejected a pro-Western orientation. Although Israel is a key

(TABLE 11 continued).

	QATAR	UAE	OMAN
Population (millions)	3	1.4	1.3
Gross National Product (GNP)* ($ billions)	6	24	7.5
Defense Expenditures* (as % of GNP)	3.5	7.9	27.9
Total Military Manpower	6,000	43,000	22,000
Army (selected indicators)	1 royal guard brigade: 1 tank battalion, 3 infantry battalions, 1 artillery battery 1 SAM battery (Rapier) Tanks: 24 AMX–30	1 royal guard brigade 1 armored brigade 1 mechanized infantry brigade 2 infantry brigades 1 artillery brigade	1 royal guard brigade 1 armored regiment 2 light field artillery regiments 8 infantry regiments 1 parachute regiment Tanks: 6 M–60 A–1, 27 Chieftain
Navy (selected indicators)	3 fast-attack craft 6 patrol craft	6 fast-attack craft 9 patrol craft	7 fast-attack craft 4 patrol craft
Air Force (selected indicators)	9 fighter ground-attack aircraft 11 helicopters 5 SAM (Tigercat)	1 squadron fighter ground-attack aircraft 2 squadrons interceptors 47 helicopters	2 squadrons fighter ground-attack aircraft 1 squadron fighter ground-attack reconnaissance aircraft 2 squadrons helicopters AAM: AIM–9

Sources: *The Military Balance, 1985–1986* (London: International Institute for Strategic Studies, 1985); *World Military Expenditures and Arms Transfers, 1985* (Washington, D.C.: U.S. Arms Control and Disarmament Agency, 1985); Anthony Cordesman, *The Gulf and the Search for Strategic Stability* (Boulder, Colo.: Westview Press, 1984).

Note: The army, navy, and air-force listings present a profile of military capability noting only those weapons and systems that the author regards as key indicators of military power.

*Estimates of GNP and defense expenditures are based on 1983 data.

U.S. regional ally, its military contribution is not included here, since the discussion is limited to gulf states.

In the global ranking of regional arms races the Persian Gulf looms very large, not as measured by absolute military capability (which is comparatively small) but in terms of the pace of militarization. The race, which accelerated after the British withdrawal in the early 1970s, has been led by the Saudis. Saudi Arabia is the largest Western-aligned military power in the region, with an armed force of 62,500 supported by a population of 8 million.[132] (Table 11 compares the military resources of the conservative gulf states.) However, the Saudi military is only the third largest in the region. It is dwarfed by the resources of Iran and Iraq, the two largest hostile regional military powers, with armed forces of 305,000 and 520,000, respectively. (See Table 12.)

There is a large gap between the West's principal surrogate, Saudi Arabia, and those of the other five GCC states. Qatar, the smallest of the six, fields an armed force of only 6,000 drawn from a total population of 300,000. Its air force includes less than 12 combat aircraft, and its navy must rely principally on only 6 patrol craft. The disparity in military capability and resources between the two primary hostile states, Iran and Iraq, and the conservative gulf states is great; without Saudi Arabia the gulf states would be in greater difficulty than they are. For this reason, the Persian Gulf states must take some comfort in the fact that the Iran-Iraq War diverts attention and resources from any military ambitions that Iraqi President Saddam Hussein and/or the Ayatollah Khomeini might have in the southern Arabian peninsula. The southern gulf states are somewhat isolated from the north; the land routes connecting the two theaters are underdeveloped and easily blocked. However, projection of air and naval power against the south is an easier task logistically and tactically. Air assaults—particularly against oil terminals and storage facilities—remain the primary security threat and concern of the gulf nations.

Although the smaller gulf states clearly possess the financial resources to construct an adequate defense, large strategic problems constrain a regional strategy. First, there is virtually no interoperability of equipment and weapons among the forces of the GCC nations, despite plans designed to correct such shortcomings. In that sense, there is little collective security consciousness. The meager air-defense assets among the states are not linked, and there is little joint military exercising of air or naval forces. Second, these nations have generally not formulated plans that would create a common policy of defense procurement; weapons systems are often acquired in a piecemeal fashion. Third, the manpower ratios for virtually all of the GCC nations are very low. This is an acute problem for regional air forces.[133]

It is, however, the problem of security partnership that is most severe. The GCC provides little more than the theoretical matrix for defense cooperation. Not the least of the formidable political obstacles preventing a genuine defense union in this region is the intermittent but effective negative pressure exerted by Iran and Iraq on Saudi Arabia. Neither Baghdad nor Tehran wish for the GCC to become anything more than a consultative body, in much the same way that the Soviet Union hopes the Western European Union—which seeks to create a European defense confederation—will probably remain an impotent institution.

TABLE 12
Hostile Gulf Balance (1985–1986)

	IRAN	IRAQ	NORTH YEMEN	SOUTH YEMEN
Population (millions)	43	15	8	2.2
Gross National Product (GNP)ᵃ ($ billions)	122.6	31	3	1.02
Defense Expendituresᵃ (as % of GNP)	5.0	47.2	15.4	17.4
Total Military Manpower	305,000ᵇ	520,000	35,000	27,000
Army (selected indicators)	3 mechanized divisions 7 infantry divisions 1 air brigade Tanks: 1,800 (T–54, T–55, T–62, T–72, Chieftain, M–47, M–48, M–60)	6 armored divisions 5 mechanized motorized infantry divisions 5 infantry divisions 4 mountain divisions Tanks: 3,000 (T–54, T–55, T–62, T–72, Chieftain)	1 armored brigade 1 mechanized brigade 5 infantry brigades 3 artillery brigades Tanks: 650 (T–34, T–54, T–55, M–60)	1 armored brigade 1 mechanized brigade 10 infantry brigades 1 artillery brigade Tanks: 450 (T–54, T–55, T–62)
Navy (selected indicators)	3 destroyers 4 frigates 1 corvette 7 fast-attack craft 7 patrol craft	1 frigate 15 fast-attack craft 11 patrol craft 3 amphibious vessels	6 fast-attack craft 9 patrol craft 11 transports 35 helicopters AAM: AIM–9	10 fast-attack craft 6 patrol craft 7 amphibious vessels
Air Force (selected indicators)	8 squadrons fighter ground-attack aircraft (F–4, F–5) 20 interceptors/fighter ground-attack aircraft 65 helicopters 5 squadrons SAM (Rapier)	2 squadrons bombers 11 squadrons fighter ground-attack aircraft 5 squadrons interceptors ASM: Exocet	5 squadrons fighters	4 squadrons fighter ground-attack aircraft 3 squadrons interceptors 1 squadron helicopters ASM: Sagger

Sources: The Military Balance, 1985–1986 (London: International Institute for Strategic Studies, 1985); World Military Expenditures and Arms Transfers, 1985 (Washington, D.C.: U.S. Arms Control and Disarmament Agency, 1985); Anthony Cordesman, The Gulf and the Search for Strategic Stability (Boulder, Colo.: Westview Press, 1984).

Note: The army, navy, and air-force listings present a profile of military capability noting only those weapons and systems that the author regards as key indicators of military power.

ᵃEstimates of GNP and defense expenditures are based on 1983 data.
ᵇEstimates of Iranian military manpower vary widely, depending on whether revolutionary guards are included. This figure includes only regular military forces.

TABLE 13
GCC Arms Transfer Payments, 1979–1983
($ millions) (current dollars)

RECIPIENT		SUPPLIER							
	Total	Soviet Union	United States	France	United Kingdom	West Germany	Italy	PRC	Other
Saudi Arabia	12,125	—	5,100	2,500	1,900	525	200	—	1,900
Kuwait	450	30	180	—	50	70	110	—	10
Bahrain	120	—	10	40	—	40	10	—	20
UAE	620	—	20	350	90	110	30	—	20
Qatar	765	—	10	440	310	—	—	—	5
Oman	565	—	80	20	430	—	10	5	20

Source: World Military Expenditures and Arms Transfers, 1985 (Washington, D.C.: U.S. Arms Control and Disarmament Agency, 1985).

Any genuine regional military capability for the GCC nations would be discouraged by hostile states in the area. This would include frustrating attempts to negotiate for U.S. naval and/or air access, as Oman has already learned.

Finally, there is the danger—peculiar to this region—that a capability to defend against external aggression will upset the delicate internal political balance in the GCC states. The governments of the region are not characterized by great stability. A potent military force could become the tool for internal repression and serve as the provocation for, or instrument of, military coups. With the exception of Saudi Arabia the military elites of these states do not rule; they are regarded with some suspicion by the population. In Saudi Arabia and Iraq the military is monitored closely by paramilitary forces to guard against the formation of independent political power bases. In sum, internal security seems to remain the prime national concern, and absent the appearance of an overt external threat—which to date has not materialized to the satisfaction of these states—the priorities are unlikely to change.

Two measures of how seriously a state regards threats to its security are defense expenditures and arms transfer agreements. A wide range of threat perception exists in the gulf, as tables 12 and 13 illustrate. In 1983 Bahrain and Kuwait devoted 4 percent of GNP to defense while the UAE expended 7.9 percent. Oman, however, expended 27.9 percent of GNP in defense-related programs, suggesting that it regards defense as a more critical need than its neighbors do.[134] Of the five smaller states, Qatar expended the largest amount for arms calculated cumulatively in current dollars. As Table 13 shows, from 1979 to 1983 Oman spent $565 million for imported arms. Bahrain devoted the smallest absolute amount at only $120 million. France and West Germany are the largest suppliers for Bahrain, while Britain is by far the dominant supplier for Oman. The United States figures as the dominant arms supplier to Kuwait, which is also the only GCC nation to receive arms from the Soviet Union.[135] Saudi Arabia purchased $12.1 billion of arms in this same period, with the United States providing 42 percent and France, 21 percent.

By contrast, during the same period Iran and Iraq received $5.3 billion in arms, cumulatively, and $17.6 billion, respectively. In the case of Iraq the Soviet Union was the major supplier, with France as the second supplier. The data available on sales to Iran are incomplete, although according to the U.S. Arms Control and Disarmament Agency, from 1979-83 the United States provided nearly 23 percent of Tehran's arms shipments.[136]

South Yemen: The Key Soviet Ally

North and South Yemen have become detached from the gulf and the Arab world primarily as the result of constant internal upheaval in and between both states. The hostility between the two nations has at times isolated southwest Arabia from the rest of the region. The recent history of the Yemens is a complicated and confusing one, with regime changes often reflecting pendulum swings in political leadership, resulting in policy fluctuations toward one or another of the two superpowers. There has, however, been one rather consistent theme in the south—a nationalist attachment to Marxist ideology, which has been encouraged by the Soviet Union and which (not surprisingly) has served as Moscow's entrée to a military presence in Arabia. By contrast, while the leadership in the north has changed with some frequency as well, Marxism has been held in some suspicion by North Yemeni leaders. San'a's policy is, therefore, often described as potentially pro-Western. The potential, however, has rarely been fulfilled, which explains the lack of enthusiasm shown by U.S. leaders in approaching San'a to construct a political-military relationship to balance that which the Soviets enjoy in Aden.

The genesis of much of the turmoil in the Yemens was the 1954 British decision to establish greater administrative control over its gulf protectorates and to form an Arabian federation. Neighboring states opposed the British plan, regarding it as an extension of British imperial policy in the gulf. At the same time the South Yemeni capital of Aden was becoming the focal point for radical leftist movements opposed to any continued British presence or control over the protectorates. The British decision to include Aden in the Southern Arabian Federation in 1963 touched off a period of civil war, characterized by fighting between competing radical groups. After British withdrawal (which included closure of the large British military base at Aden), accelerated by the 1967 civil war, a strong Marxist regime came to power in Aden. A succession of radical regimes there alarmed more moderate neighboring states, particularly Saudi Arabia and North Yemen.

Attempts by the governments in Aden and San'a to unify the two Yemens in the early 1970s met with opposition from the Saudis, who feared that unification would lead to the creation of an even stronger Marxist state on its border. As the prospects for unification waned, North Yemen's leaders began to court the Saudis in an effort to counter the military relationship between Aden and Moscow. These efforts failed and in 1968 a Soviet delegation, led by Admiral of the Fleet Sergei Gorshkov, signed a secret fifteen-year agreement with the Aden government for military and economic assistance. This agreement yielded the Soviets a naval base at Khorramshar and supporting intelligence and logistics facilities at Socotra and Mukalla. The alliance was strengthened by a 1979 twenty-year Treaty of Friendship with the Soviet Union.[137] The Soviets currently maintain a military force of about a thousand in addition to the presence of Cubans and East Germans. Periodically, Moscow has attempted to promote relations with the San'a regime.[138] The Aden government, suspicious of this development, has begun to court other benefactors, including the Soviet client states of Libya and Ethiopia.

The long history of internal rivalry in South Yemen continues to haunt the country's political process, as illustrated in the recent change of government. President Ali Nassar Muhammed al-Hassani, who had assumed power in 1980, was overthrown in January 1986 in a coup that reportedly took the lives of more than 12,000.[139] The reasons for the coup are unclear, although president Muhammed had adopted a policy of building closer ties with the West and with such neighboring moderate states as Saudia Arabia, North Yemen, and Oman, which provoked strong criticism by leaders of rival Marxist factions and caused some concern in Moscow. Suspicions of Soviet meddling in the internal struggles were fueled when a former president, Abdel Fattah Ismail (a pro-Soviet hardliner), returned from a trip to the Soviet Union in early 1985, presumably to assume control of the government from president Muhammed. However, the current interim president is Moscow-sponsored Haidar Abu Bakr al-Attas, who is locked in a power struggle with competing groups, one of which is led by Salim Saleh Mohammed, the new secretary of the Yemeni Socialist party's Central Committee.

The Soviets are likely to monitor the situation in Aden more closely in the future. Moscow was clearly surprised by the timing of the coup, although the Soviets are probably pleased at assumption of leadership by an orthodox Marxist. However, considering the strategic importance of Aden to Soviet policy in the gulf region, the Soviets can ill afford many such surprises if they threaten to weaken the Moscow-Aden military entente. The immediate impact of instability in South Yemen on the United States is difficult to assess, unless the chaos propells a pro-Western faction into national leadership.

Oman: The West's New Pillar?

Since the fall of the shah of Iran the United Sates has reassessed its security position in the Persian Gulf, concentrating primarily on a search for a new "pillar" to replace Iran. There are very few candidates, but one may be emerging—the Sultanate of Oman. Its potential strategic contribution to the West is obvious. Oman's control over Cape Musandam and the primary shipping channels in the Strait of Hormuz gives it central responsibility among all the gulf states for protecting the unimpeded passage of oil to and from the gulf. In addition, its air and naval facilities at Seeb, Salalah, Masirah, and Thumrait could serve as major staging points for U.S. forces. In this regard, Oman acts as an effective Western counterweight to South Yemen, the only avowedly Marxist state in the gulf, and the largest Soviet base in the region. In fact, Oman is the only gulf state that has signed formal access rights agreements with Washington, although Somalia and Kenya have reportedly agreed to allow prepositioning of equipment on their soil.

Finally, unlike the other five GCC nations, Oman is to date the only gulf state unaffected by the Shiite revolution in the region. As a result, it is insulated from Iranian threats of sociopolitical destabilization, which have at times concerned its GCC neighbors, Kuwait and the UAE. In addition, Oman has wisely refrained from overtly allying itself with Iran or Iraq in the ongoing gulf war. Oman's leader, Sultan Qaboos, has also gained the respect of his neighbors—allies and adversaries—in crushing the only serious threat to his regime, the South Yemen-backed Dhofar rebellion of 1965–75. Qaboos's skill has been recognized by Aden, whose leader was forced to sign a peace agreement with Qaboos in 1982 that ended the attempts by the Popular Front for the Liberation of Oman (PFLO) to destabilize his government.

Oman is the only gulf state whose military forces have had recent combat experience, which also happened to have been successful. Oman's forces are small but impressive. Qaboos has retained over 200 British military advisers, who have built a military force of 21,500, commanded by a British general whose past responsibilities included command of all United Kingdom land forces. A number of Pakistani military advisers are also retained by the sultan. Further, unlike other gulf states, Oman has been able to reduce dependency on foreign soldiers by training an Omani officer corps to command its troops.

Oman's military force (outlined in Table 11) includes 1 Royal guard brigade, 1 armored regiment, 2 light field artillery regiments, and 8 infantry regiments. Its navy has 4 shore patrol craft and 7 fast-attack vessels equipped with French Exocet surface-to-surface missiles (SSM). The sultan's air force includes 52 combat aircraft, 2 helicopter squadrons and a stockpile of 250 AIM–9 Sidewinder air-to-air missiles (AAM).[140]

The expected acquisition of Rapier surface-to-air missiles and Blindfire radar systems will provide the Omanis with an integrated all-weather air-defense capability as well. Furthermore, although the Omani land combat force is primarily light infantry, it is gradually acquiring an antiarmor capability by replacing aging Russian-supplied equipment with U.S.-built TOW antitank weapons. This antiarmor capability will probably be sufficient to mount an attack, considering the logistical and geographic obstacles that the only likely adversary (South Yemen) would face in deploying armor on the border.

The navy is the weakest link in Oman's military force, although it has performed well in at least one test in September 1980 at the outbreak of the Iran-Iraq War, when the small Omani naval force repelled 3 Iranian frigates in the Strait of Hormuz. The naval threat to Oman may well become the most serious military problem for the Qaboos government. Should Iran prevail in the gulf conflict, the Khomeini regime is likely to seek to reassert its control over the Strait of Hormuz and possibly its claim to Cape Musandam. An end to hostilities with Iraq would allow Khomeini to focus his naval force against Oman. In addition, the land threat from South Yemen cannot be discounted, particularly since Qaboos maintains only 1 brigade to patrol the border, opposite 3 South Yemeni brigades. However, South Yemen's readiness is reportedly only 30 percent to 40 percent of total potential.[141]

Oman has been the catalyst for a more effective regional defense network since the GCC's inauguration in 1981. It also cooperated with the U.S. RDJTF over the last five years during joint troop exercises. Most significantly from a political standpoint, Qaboos has allowed the United States to improve military facilities at four sites in Oman as part of a $320 million military improvement agreement, which is separate from the U.S. military aid program for Oman.[142] The improvements include runway modernization; petroleum, oil, and lubricant storage; and aircraft parking and maintenance. In addition, prepositioning of stocks for U.S. air operations in the region has also been allowed.[143] The key to this effort is U.S. access to, and improvement of, Masirah, which when completed will give Oman a strategically located air base out of range for most Iranian and South Yemeni combat aircraft.

Oman's close military relationship with Washington (reaffirmed by Vice President Bush's trip to Oman in May 1984) has not been without risk to the sultan's political position in the region. The leaders of Syria, South Yemen, Iran, and Libya have all threatened Qaboos with retribution for his decision to allow limited U.S. air and naval access to Omani facilities. Should these four nations band together in a concerted attempt to topple Qaboos, the United States would lose the only credibly armed, assertively pro–United States nation in the gulf. An attempt to overthrow Qaboos could be made easier with the assistance of several thousand Soviet and Soviet-bloc personnel, scattered throughout the region.

Qaboos's overtures to Washington may have begun to alienate the UAE and Kuwait, who have criticized the U.S.-Omani alliance. For this reason, Qaboos has sought to keep any U.S. presence as invisible as possible. The effectiveness of this policy is limited, and without Saudi support—which to date has not been evident—Qaboos may find himself increasingly isolated within the GCC. Should he become a political pariah, his ability to continue supporting a pro–United States policy may be impeded.

12.
SUPERPOWER RIVALRY IN THE PERSIAN GULF

The Soviet Shadow

Soviet Objectives

The December 1979 Soviet invasion of Afghanistan forced many to revise previous estimates of Soviet intentions in the region. Some have argued, however, that despite the Afghanistan campaign, the Soviets would be reluctant to "commit military forces to an area of the world where American interests by and large predominate."[144] Others have emphasized that the Soviet Union does possess certain geographical advantages that allow them "a permanent presence that the West can match only with great difficulty."[145]

While there is much debate over how the Soviets might evaluate the climate for intervention, there is general agreement on the event that would precipitate such an initiative—the destabilization of Iran. Clearly, Soviet influence in Iran has increased over the last several years. This has been due, in part, to Iran's 1981 decision to accept Soviet security assistance in the hope of lessening the economic drain caused by internal unrest and the expensive war with Iraq.[146] From 1979 to 1983 Iran received $975 million in arms from the Soviet Union. The Soviets are interested in radicalizing the regime in Tehran and hope to influence the direction of internal political movements. Although Moscow was initially reluctant to criticize publicly the Khomeini government, recent Soviet statements suggest growing dissatisfaction with the Shiite regime.[147]

Certainly, the Soviets have the capability to intervene militarily if Moscow determines that Khomeini is straying from the straight and narrow. Although the Afghanistan invasion is not totally analogous, one can envision a similar situation in which a pro-Moscow faction offers an "invitation" to the Soviets to intervene and "stabilize" the regime. Regardless of the internal political situation, Soviet control over Iranian oil fields is an attractive inducement for Soviet pressure. As one analyst has noted, the Soviets have not overtly threatened to control the flow of Persian Gulf oil, but they have concluded agreements with, and have sent advisers to, those countries that "sit astride the oil sea lanes of communication—the People's Democratic Republic of Yemen, Ethiopia, Libya, and Afghanistan."[148]

Ultimately, the Soviets would like to accelerate the erosion of U.S. influence in the gulf and possibly replace the United States as the superpower protector of the region. The Soviets realize that they need do little to encourage the already virulent anti-Western proclivities of many Arab states. Potential Western allies in the region are at least skeptical about a visible alliance with the United States.

Furthermore, Moscow seeks to offer an alternative security framework that would minimize domestic protest for those states seeking a superpower relationship. The late Soviet president Leonid Brezhnev suggested that Moscow would be able to meet the security concerns of regional states, guaranteeing the uninterrupted flow of Persian Gulf oil without the less attractive political side effects that would accompany a Western alliance.[149] This declaration was followed by a more structured proposal in December 1980 during Brezhnev's state visit to India.[150] None of Brezhnev's successors—Yuri Andropov, Konstantin Chernenko, or Mikhail Gorbachev—has ever resurrected the proposal, although Gorbachev used the occasion of the Chernenko funeral to warn Pakistani President Mohammed Zia ul-Haq against continuing assistance to the Mujahedeen in Afghanistan.

Soviet Intervention Capabilities

Soviet intervention forces for the Persian Gulf/Southwest Asian area would be drawn from the southern theater (TVD), one of the five major Soviet strategic regions. The southern theater includes the north Caucasus, Transcaucasus, and Turkestan military districts (MD) in addition to Afghanistan, which is treated as a separate MD. The headquarters for the southern theater is Tashkent.

The Soviets have committed 28 motorized rifle divisions, 1 tank division, and 1 airborne division to this region, although only a fraction of these forces would be committed to the gulf theater at any one time.[151] Presumably, if the Soviets intended to strike quickly to gain the advantage of surprise, airborne divisions would be deployed as the first wave of an interventionary force. The total Soviet airborne strength is

8 divisions, which include 1 training division. Currently, one airborne division is deployed in Afghanistan, leaving six available for deployment elsewhere. Excluding the 4 regiments of ground-attack aircraft committed to Afghanistan, the southern TVD has 9 regiments of tactical aviation and part of one medium-range bomber squadron in addition to a number of committed Backfire bombers. The Soviets have substantially improved the tactical air forces in this theater, increasing the number of SU–24 Fencer deep-strike aircraft and replacing older models. MIG–23 and MIG–27 aircraft would also be deployed. The ground-attack mission seems to have predominated over the air-defense mission in Soviet regional security planning since 1980.

Soviet naval forces could be drawn from several fleets, depending on the contingency.[152] That force could include vessels from the Caspian Flotilla, a small deployment of only 5 principal combatants and about 30 minor combatants. The Soviet Indian Ocean Fleet includes 20–25 vessels with port facilities at Aden and in Ethiopia. The Soviets have additional naval and air facilities in Syria and Libya. Naval forces from the Soviet Fifth Escadra deployed in the Mediterranean could also be employed, although they might be reserved for a southern flank contingency.

Soviet amphibious forces in the region are considerable. The Soviet Black Sea Fleet (which deploys amphibious forces into the Mediterranean) includes 20–25 LST/LSM vessels, a larger force than is found in any of the other Soviet fleets.

In addition, 2–3 amphibious vessels are regularly deployed in the Mediterranean, carrying several hundred troops. Finally, the Black Sea Fleet (a component command of the southwestern TVD) has a naval infantry brigade of 3,000 marines, heavily equipped with armored personnel carriers, artillery, and a small number of tanks.[153] Naval infantry units in all Soviet fleets have been increased in recent years.

The Soviet Union would be able to deploy an impressive military force should it decide to intervene in the Persian Gulf/Southwest Asia. There is great debate about the likely Soviet invasion route in any military campaign in this region, although there is a consensus that Iran would most probably be the target of such an operation. Of the divisions available in the southern theater, roughly 13 are close enough to the border to be deployed into Iran with some dispatch. Invading Soviet divisions would have to travel roughly 300 miles to reach Tehran and 650 miles to reach the oil fields at Abadan.[154] Although the journey would not proceed over a superhighway, the Soviets have invested considerably in upgrading the road and rail network north of Iran and Afghanistan.[155] The Soviets were able to make good use of this network during the December 1979 invasion of Afghanistan, deploying 85,000 troops within the first weeks of the operation, supported by an additional 30,000 from across the border.[156] In addition to the use of maximum firepower and mechanization, the Soviet forces deployed in Afghanistan were also equipped for chemical warfare. Evidence has continued to mount on the use of chemical and biological agents during the Soviet occupation.[157] In addition to the development of infrastructure along the Iranian and Afghan borders the Soviets have invested in similar projects in the Gulf of Aden—Ethiopia and South Yemen—including airfield improvements, naval repair facilities, command and control headquarters, and port construction.[158] The Soviets could also support nuclear conflict in the region, utilizing Backfire bombers based in the Transcaucasus region and SS–20 missiles, some of which are almost definitely deployed to target portions of southwest Asia.

Most analysts assume the Soviets would seek to control all of Iran and would make their plans with this objective in mind. However, as with the southern flank (discussed in Part 1 of this study), the Soviets might seize only a small amount of territory; they might seek an area where they are less likely to encounter U.S. opposition because of the combination of Soviet surprise and the lack of in-theater U.S. military forces.[159]

U.S. Policy Objectives and Priorities

Theater Priorities

The U.S. Department of Defense (DOD) has identified three theaters that are "of most critical interest to it—Europe, the Middle East and Southwest Asia, and East Asia and the Pacific."[160] The strategic assumptions upon which this definition of "critical interest" is based implicitly rejects the notion that the United States will *most likely* be faced with the classic Western security challenge—a Soviet conventional attack in central Europe. It recognizes that the Soviet strategy may be evolving to take advantage of a global power projection force, and thus while Europe remains the focal point for East-West tensions, Moscow may be looking more than in the past to political-military opportunities on the "fringe," (that is, NATO's flanks and the Persian Gulf). Thus, Moscow's "fringe strategy" has perhaps begun to refocus the U.S. strategic concern to take greater account of the Western military position in these theaters. For example, the *FY 1985 Report of the Secretary of Defense to the U.S. Congress* (released in February 1984) states in a categorical fashion that "the primary objective of our policy for the Middle East is to deter Soviet aggression in that vital area."[161]

While not representing a radical departure from previous U.S. policy declarations on Middle East strategy, a review of previous annual DOD reports reveals that the secretary of defense has rarely—if ever—identified resistance of "Soviet aggression" as the major U.S. policy goal for that region. For example, an examination of the two earlier annual reports shows that, even during an administration that has emphasized the primacy of the Soviet global threat in U.S. strategic planning, the categorical and specific reference to the Middle East in the FY 1985 report is new. In the FY 1984 statement Secretary of Defense Caspar Weinberger, in referring to U.S. vital interests in the Near East/South Asia, stated that U.S. objectives in this region are

> . . . to preserve and protect the independence of states in the region, including both Israel and friendly Arab nations, from aggression and subversion; to help secure a lasting peace for all the peoples of the Mideast; to prevent the spread of Soviet influence and the consequent loss of freedom and independence it entails, and to protect Western access to the energy resources of the area, and to maintain the security of key sea lanes to this region.[162]

In one year concern over Soviet influence and aggression was catapulted from the third objective in a list of five to the primary objective. The FY 1986 and FY 1987 DOD reports continue the emphasis on deterring Soviet expansion in the region. Although one could quibble about the 1984 report's terminology (that is, its references to the Middle East and Southwest Asia), the "Regional Objectives" section does not distinguish between the two terms and in fact treats them as one theater. This is not the case in the FY 1985 report, which lists U.S. objectives in Southwest Asia separately and does not include among them an explicit reference to Soviet aggression, although it does list the prevention of "influence or takeover by forces inimical to our interests" as the first of four U.S. options in Southwest Asia.[163] One could debate whether this rather broad statement is designed to encompass both external and internal challenges to U.S. interests.

The national-security bureaucracy has resisted attempts to differentiate between the terms "Middle East" and "Southwest Asia" in documents that discuss security planning for the region.[164] Further, although the term "Persian Gulf" is often used as a generic label to refer to much of the Middle East, the eight gulf states do comprise a key strategic subregion. Three of the riparians—Iran, Iraq, and Saudi Arabia—constitute nearly 95 percent of the gulf population; the balance live in what Middle East scholar J. C. Hurewitz has termed the "ministates"—Bahrain, Kuwait, Qatar, Oman, and the United Arab Emirates.

The strategic meaning of the term "Persian Gulf" has become somewhat blurred, as the geographic context has been broadened to include reference to Southwest Asia. Such reference principally incorporates in the discussion such states as Pakistan, considered to be key to U.S. policy in the area. The principal economic concern remains focused on the eight gulf states and their oil fields, which produce the petroleum critical for the economic health of many Western nations.

U.S. policy in the gulf has been described in terms somewhat different from those used to explain U.S. interests in Southwest Asia or the Middle East. The major concern of the United States in the gulf has been to insulate the politically fragile riparians from outside forces, to "assist the peoples of the region to pursue their legitimate aspirations free of outside pressure," while realizing that "the friendly states of the Gulf are fully engaged both in the geopolitical dynamics of the strategically important Gulf region and in the political dynamics of the broader Arab and Islamic worlds."[165] The Reagan administration has sought to reorient U.S. policy toward the gulf, "placing a new emphasis on the military or security aspect, bringing it more into balance with the economic and political elements of this policy."[166] That new emphasis recognizes a range of threats to the stability of the gulf states, emphasizing the need to develop a "capability to project military force toward the region as a deterrent to outside pressure against those friendly states."[167]

In addition to creating a unified command for the region, the Reagan administration has made two concrete policy decisions that support the concept of regional deterrence—the deployment of AWACS to bolster Saudi Arabian air defense and the five-year military aid package (which will expire shortly) for Pakistan, each of which represented part of a two-pronged policy of: (1) increased security assistance for key Western-oriented states in the region; and (2) the deployment of U.S. military hardware to project the U.S. intention of underwriting the security of regional surrogates. In addition, the Reagan administration has confirmed its belief that in order to protect the gulf sheikhdoms it is necessary first to identify those states peripheral to the gulf that in time of crisis might be prevailed upon to support Western policy—Pakistan, Jordan, and Israel.

Finally, the administration recognizes that any U.S. attempt to "protect" states in the region can be successful only if pursued without the traditional instruments of Great Power diplomacy. As former assistant secretary of state for Near East and South Asian affairs Nicholas Veliotes stated in his 1982 testimony before a joint congressional hearing, "We well understand the sensitivities in the region to treaties or formal alliances with outside powers." Unfortunately, the Soviet Union is not so constrained in erecting a series of security alliances with regional states, as evidenced by the increasing Soviet presence in South Yemen and Ethiopia and the de facto formation of a pro-Soviet entente among Libya, South Yemen, Ethiopia, and Syria.

U.S. Confrontations with Libya

In March and April of 1986 a combination of factors led to a series of military confrontations involving U.S. and Libyan forces. The incidents are instructive for a number of reasons, not the least of which is the inauguration—marked by these incidents—of a new component to the Reagan Doctrine, which seems designed to legitimize the use of U.S. military force to combat threats other than the classic East-West confrontations that often preoccupy U.S. strategists. The Libyan confrontations bring together a number of issues that will increase the importance of the Persian Gulf/Mediterranean regions: combating international terrorism, asserting the rights of maritime navigation, and limiting the expansionist tendencies of Soviet-aligned states in the region.

In late March 1986 the U.S. Sixth Fleet began planned naval maneuvers in the Mediterranean, which were intended to challenge the legitimacy of Libya's claim that the entire 150,000 square miles of the Gulf of Sidra fell within Libyan territorial waters. Libyan leader Colonel Muammar Quaddafi had announced in 1973 that in addition to the standard 12-mile zone of territorial waters recognized by international convention, Libya had drawn a line across the mouth of the Gulf of Sidra at 32 degrees, 30 minutes north latitude, which extends roughly from the city of Misurata on the western shore of the gulf to Benghazi on the eastern shore.

The United States has long objected to Qaddafi's self-proclaimed "line of death." The legal argument against the line rests on the 1958 Convention on the Territorial Sea and Contiguous Zone, which carefully defined the conditions under which a nation may extend its internal waters. The Gulf of Sidra does not fall within these conditions. Libya is not a signatory to this convention and, therefore, does not feel bound by it. The United States and most Western nations recognize only a 12-mile coastal limit, which would place most of the Gulf of Sidra within international waters.

The United States has disputed Libya's territorial claims but until 1981 had not actively challenged them. In August 1981 2 U.S. navy F–14 fighters shot down 2 Libyan SU–22 fighters over the gulf (60 miles off the Libyan coast) after being fired on by them. The United States claimed that its aircraft were over international waters at the time of the incident, while Libya claimed they were in Libyan territory. U.S. combat aircraft have crossed the 32° 30′ line on seven occasions since that incident.

In January 1986, as the United States was assembling a naval task force for maneuvers in the Mediterranean, Qaddafi boarded an armed Libyan patrol boat and sailed into the gulf to meet the U.S. task force and challenge the right of U.S. warships to violate his proclaimed line of death. Qaddafi was deterred by the size of the U.S. force, and there was no military confrontation.

In March 1986 U.S. and Libyan forces clashed in the gulf as a 3-carrier, 30-ship, U.S. naval task force was conducting planned maneuvers. The United States, announcing that it was simply asserting its "ability to defend the free world's interests"[168] ordered ships of the Sixth Fleet across the 32° 30' line. Libyan aircraft fired on the U.S. vessels, using Soviet-supplied SAM-2 and SAM-5 missiles. The weapons missed their targets, but U.S. carrier-based A–6 and A–7 aircraft responded by sinking 2 Libyan patrol craft and destroying a SAM radar site. The U.S. vessels penetrated to within 40 miles of the Libyan coast, halfway into the gulf itself, but well outside the 12-mile territorial limit.

Although the Reagan administration justified the attack as a necessary challenge to an illegal territorial declaration, mounting evidence of Libyan complicity in a number of recent terrorist incidents in which Americans were among the targets clearly contributed to the timing of the naval exercise. In late April 1986 elements of the U.S. Sixth Fleet again entered the gulf to attack Libya in reprisal for terrorist incidents. The administration claimed to have intercepted communications between the Libyan embassy in East Berlin and the government in Tripoli that implicated Libyan officials in the bombing of a nightclub in West Berlin known to be frequented by U.S. servicemen.

U.S. aircraft hit targets in Tripoli and Benghazi, including Qaddafi's headquarters at the Aziziya barracks. The attack involved carrier-based A–6, A–7, F–14, and F–18 fighters as well as F–111 bombers based in Great Britain. EF–111 and E–A6B aircraft were employed to jam Libyan radar networks. The attack was a success, but it was complicated logistically by the refusal of the French and Spanish governments to permit the F–111s to overfly their territory en route to their targets. This necessitated four separate in-flight refueling operations and added over 1,000 miles to a 2,800 mile journey.

The Libyan raids raise a number of policy questions for the United States and its European allies. The attacks brought to the surface a number of simmering disputes. Clearly, there is great disagreement between Washington and the NATO capitals over a number of emerging security issues, some of which will affect allied policy in the Mediterranean and the Persian Gulf. The concern over Qaddafi's policies has raised larger issues: how to deal effectively with governments that lend official support to terrorists, how and whether to employ military force against "low-level" threats, and to what extent the United States should act unilaterally when the support of its European allies is not forthcoming. In the Libyan case allied naval and air units could have contributed valuably to the operation. Granting of overflight (which was denied in at least two instances) and permission to use NATO operating bases in allied countries (which was not requested by Washington for fear of a very public "no") would have reduced the logistical "tail" of the Libyan operation to much smaller proportions. In addition, had the Libyan operation been multilateral, the political effect would have been enhanced considerably. So long as the United States is forced to act unilaterally, the impression that NATO is unable to act in concert will be reinforced.

The Libyan crisis also reminded NATO leaders that perhaps the nature of the challenges to Alliance cohesion are changing. A new form of political-military threat is emerging that could eclipse the threat from the Warsaw Pact. The more often the United States acts unilaterally, the more unlikely it is that the allies can be persuaded to contribute to operations that West European leaders would find politically difficult to support.

One disturbing aspect of the Libyan crisis is the consistent level of Soviet support for Qaddafi's policies. Clearly, the Soviet Union was careful not to congratulate publicly Qaddafi for his line-of-death proclamation, and there is no evidence that Moscow actively aided Qaddafi during the March and April attacks against U.S. naval forces. Nevertheless, without Soviet-supplied arms, Qaddafi would be unable to implement many of his policies. Without Soviet support for Libyan terrorist cells, Qaddafi would find it more difficult to terrorize Europe as he has for the last several years. It is unclear whether Moscow privately applauded Qaddafi's Sidra declaration, although there is some strain between Moscow and Tripoli. The Soviets are reportedly more reluctant than in the past to resupply Libyan forces with sophisticated military hardware.[169] Should the Soviet Union move closer to Qaddafi and solidify a military relationship (similar to that which is evolving in Syria), the effect on NATO could be devastating. Unlimited Soviet access to Libyan bases (so far denied by Qaddafi) would allow Moscow to challenge the U.S. Sixth Fleet. Soviet use of the former U.S. air base (Wheelus) or the former British base at al-Adem, would provide a strategic foothold from which to threaten U.S. and allied forces in the entire Mediterranean basin.

Presently, the Soviets have only limited access to Libyan facilities, under agreements reached between Qaddafi's deputy Abdel Salem Jalloud and Soviet Marshal Grechko. Subsequent agreements between Moscow and Tripoli have brought MIG–25 aircraft to Libya, the first state outside the Soviet bloc to receive them. In addition to sophisticated weaponry, there are more than 2,000 Soviet military personnel in Libya and a large number of other Soviet-bloc personnel. Libyan facilities have also been used by Soviet aircraft as refueling points en route to resupply Soviet-supported forces in Angola and Mozambique.

It is difficult to gauge the current state of Libyan-Soviet relations. While Moscow has been less supportive publicly of Qaddafi's terrorist campaign, Soviet officials have not criticized Qaddafi's anti-Western statements. The Soviets must be concerned about the erratic nature of Qaddafi's policies. Mikhail Gorbachev cannot risk a closer relationship with Qaddafi until it is clear that Qaddafi has crushed any internal attempts to topple him. Qaddafi's support from his own military, for example, has not always been firm. In addition, the Soviets may be wary of a closer relationship with Tripoli in light of recent upheavals in another Soviet-allied country, South Yemen, and until Gorbachev is able to gauge the future of his relations with Syria's President Assad, who is also under great internal pressure.

In sum, whether alone or in concert with the Soviet Union, Muammar Qaddafi threatens to create pressure within NATO, either because his actions directly threaten the Alliance's strategic position in the Mediterranean or because his policies could create political wedges between Washington and the European capitals, as the allies publicly disagree on how to respond. Regardless, Libya must be considered as a dangerous wild card in a region that can ill afford surprises.

Power Projection and the RDF

The invasion of Afghanistan raised important questions about how best to cope with "non-NATO contingencies"—political-military crises that occur outside of the NATO formal treaty boundary. Early in the Carter administration, secretary of defense Harold Brown directed the analytical staff of the office of the secretary of defense to prepare a classified study that evaluated future U.S. foreign-policy aims and choices and focused on the utility of general purpose forces as instruments of national-security policy. This document, *Presidential Review Memorandum 10* (PRM 10), considered among the most controversial in the Carter administration's defense planning scheme, has been discussed in detail by others and will not be repeated here. For the purposes of this discussion it is sufficient to say that PRM 10 included a series of recommendations on how conventional forces might be utilized in non-NATO contingencies. The original concept was to construct flexible forces capable of operating independently of allied basing facilities. The Persian Gulf was one of three areas suggested for such forces. Planning was fairly advanced by the time of the January 1979 Iranian revolution and allowed president Carter to announce on October 1, 1979, the formation of a Rapid Deployment Force (RDF) with headquarters at MacDill Air Force Base in Tampa, Florida. Defense guidance was issued for the formation of a new command formally referred to as the Rapid Deployment Forces Joint Task Force (RDJTF).

As the RDJTF concept took shape, a multitude of serious logistical difficulties became obvious as the task of moving forces (12,000 nautical miles by sea or 8,000 nautical miles by air) became clear. The Pentagon decided to alter the concept of the RDF to a force that could operate in a "permissive environment" that required some reliance on regional facilities, including airfields and ports. The Reagan administration enthusiastically adopted the RDJTF, accelerating the appropriations designated for its development. In March 1982 then–assistant secretary of defense Francis J. West, Jr., discussed the Reagan administration's concept of the RDJTF. Its mission, according to West, is to

> . . . conduct planning, joint training, exercising and be prepared to deploy designated forces to the Southwest Asia region. The RDJTF is programmed to counter the most serious threat to the area, which would be a Soviet invasion of Iran.[170]

West noted that other missions were on the DOD list of priorities for the RDJTF, including: (1) the security of Israel and the continuation of the peace process; (2) support for the moderate states of Saudi Arabia, Oman, Jordan, and Egypt against overt attack by radical states; (3) support for moderate states against internal disorders and subversion; (4) the limitation of Soviet military influence/leverage in the region; and (5) deterrence of a Soviet invasion of the gulf.[171]

The above menu presents a formidable list of challenges for U.S. security policy, and the Reagan administration fully realizes that current funding for the RDJTF is insufficient for the task. Further, it has publicly recognized that although the RDJTF's primary theater of operations would be Southwest Asia, the United States presently lacks any

> . . . agreements to station our combat forces ashore in the area and, therefore, [can] maintain only a limited sea-based presence there. . . .
>
> The continuing Soviet occupation of Afghanistan, the Iran-Iraq war, and lower-level intraregional disputes, such as those between North and South Yemen, exemplify the range of regional instabilities that complicate our policy and strategy. Our programs for the region must therefore offer capabilities across a spectrum of potential conflicts.[172]

The Reagan administration has upgraded the RDJTF and in January 1983 created for the first time in over 35 years a new geographic unified command, with the commander of the RDJTF becoming commander of

TABLE 14
CENTCOM Force Profile*

ARMY	AIR FORCE
1 airborne division	7 tactical fighter wings
1 airmobile/air assault division	
1 mechanized infantry division	
1 light infantry division	
1 air cavalry brigade	

MARINE CORPS	NAVY
1-1/3 marine amphibious force**	3 carrier battle groups
	1 surface action group
	5 maritime patrol air squadrons

*CENTCOM has recently established a forward headquarters element (FHE) afloat with naval forces in the Persian Gulf.
**Includes a reinforced marine division and marine aircraft wing.

Source: FY 1986 DOD Annual Report to the Congress (Washington, D.C.: GPO, 1986), 231.

the U.S. Central Command (CENTCOM). In FY 1984 DOD programmed the RDJTF to include 3-1/3 army divisions, 1-1/3 marine amphibious forces, 7 air-force tactical fighter wings, and up to 3 navy carrier battle groups.[173] In addition to the FY 1986 increase in CENTCOM forces (shown in Table 14), a force of 18 chartered near-term prepositioning ships (NTPS) will carry equipment and supplies in sufficient quantities to sustain the RDJTF until the arrival of additional material from the United States. In FY 1986 additional upgrades to prepositioning have been made, including the maritime prepositioning ships (MPS) program, which will involve chartering 13 vessels, loaded with equipment for 3 marine amphibious brigades (MAB). The first MPS task force was deployed in the Atlantic in 1985. The remaining 2 were to be deployed in the Southwest Asian region and the Pacific in 1986.[174]

Agreements have been signed between the United States and regional states to preposition matériel and to utilize certain facilities in time of crisis. Prominent among these is an agreement with the government of Oman to improve selected airfields and support facilities. The Omanis have been more forthcoming during base negotiations than most states in the region. As noted earlier, other accords have been signed with Somalia and Kenya.[175]

There has been much debate about the time required to deploy CENTCOM forces to the Persian Gulf region. Although advance elements of the force—a battalion of the Eighty-second Airborne Division for example—could be lifted to the region in forty-eight to seventy-two hours, at least twenty-one days would be required to deploy a full division. The goal as stated by DOD is to "deploy a major joint task force and required support within six weeks of being asked for assistance."[176]

A Strategy for Military Response: Problems and Prospects

There are many difficulties with developing the capability to intervene militarily in Southwest Asia. The greatest uncertainty is the United States' willingness to divert forces from Europe to Southwest Asia, particularly during a period when a crisis in the gulf may be accompanied by tensions in Europe. Because of the central front bias (discussed in Part 1 of this study), little attention has been given to questions of defending the gulf without draining resources from the European theater. As the noted strategist Albert Wohlstetter has written, the lack of serious attention was due in part to the mistaken belief that

> . . . protection of alliance interests in the Persian Gulf would not call for any exercise of American or alliance power: the Russians would not risk intervention in so vital a spot for the Western alliance and the contending regional forces would balance out.[177]

As Wohlstetter pointed out, however, the demands that would be placed upon the Alliance in any gulf contingency would be quite different from those faced in central Europe, due to the lack of established infrastructure, the complex interstate rivalries, potentially greatest urgencies, and other complicating factors unique to the gulf region. Finally, as Defense Secretary Weinberger has confirmed, the troops "committed" to the newly created CENTCOM are not *exclusively* tied to it. For example, the 3-1/3 army divisions that comprise the bulk of the RDJTF combat capability are committed to NATO, and that is not expected to change in the near future.[178]

As noted earlier, access to support facilities in the gulf region is uncertain for several reasons, including the high political profile that any bilateral agreement with the United States would assume. The fact that no U.S. forces are stationed on land anywhere in the region during peacetime confirms the political sensitivity of this issue for potential host governments. The only U.S. military base in this part of the world, Diego Garcia, is 2,500 miles from the Strait of Hormuz (roughly one-week steaming time) and incapable of supporting a military force of significant size. In contrast, several in-theater facilities are available to the Soviet Union.

In the final analysis, the United States is unlikely to secure base rights within the gulf unless the host government is unusually stable and secure and is willing to accept the political risks that would attend any U.S. military presence in the region. As analyst Jeffrey Record has noted, the United States

> . . . possesses none of the critical operational and logistical benefits that it enjoys in comparative abundance in Europe, and where large U.S. military forces are firmly ensconced ashore and can count on the support of powerful and reliable allies.[179]

Nevertheless, the United States has had some success in communicating its intent to support friendly and moderate Arab states in the gulf region. The sale of AWACS to Saudi Arabia is perhaps the best example of this policy.

Despite great opposing pressure from strong lobbying groups in the United States, the Reagan administration succeeded in securing congressional approval for the AWACS deployment. The Reagan administration explained the sale as a "striking example of how we can make a contribution to the region's security in a way consistent with the political realities there."[180] During congressional hearings on the AWACS sale held in September and October 1981, the administration carefully articulated its policy on defense of the gulf region. The hearings were quite timely. The morning that former undersecretary of state James Buckley was scheduled to testify in support of the AWACS sale, 3 Iranian planes attacked several oil installations in Kuwait in reprisal for suspected Kuwaiti assistance to Iraq in its continuing conflict with Iran. The administration used this incident to illustrate the vulnerability of friendly regimes in the region to attack from radical neighbors. The sale was intended to buttress Saudi air defense and specifically to alert the Saudi air force to an impending air attack, possibly on its vast oil installations. As undersecretary Buckley explained,

> Both we and the Saudis fully realize that the air defense enhancement package we have submitted to the Congress will not enable the Saudis to defend themselves against a direct Soviet attack. Only we can do that, and only if our forces are sought and welcomed by the people and governments of the region. The proposed sale, however, will vastly enhance our ability to do so. It will, for example, insure the existence

of an extensive logistics base and support infrastructure in Saudi Arabia—including spare parts—that will facilitate rapid U.S. reinforcement in an emergency.[181]

Although the Saudis hold the key to the region's defense, they have generally been a great dissapointment to those who expected them to assume enthusiastically a larger strategic role in the gulf. As with most of the countries in this region, however, the United States inevitably expects greater contributions than the regimes are capable of withstanding. Unless and until the Saudis perceive a more immediate threat to *their* security (as opposed to a concern for U.S. interests), it is unlikely that they will make a greater military contribution to regional security.

Strategic Choices in Meeting the Threat

(The United States and the Soviet Union will continue to view the Persian Gulf as a strategic region, valuable to both sides. Although there are considerable asymmetries in the ability of the United States and Soviet Union to project military power into the region, neither nation would embark on a military campaign there without assuming some risk of reprisal. That risk is greater for the United States than for the Soviets. Nevertheless, the Soviets cannot assume that a military campaign into the Persian Gulf region will be unchallenged by the West.)

Both sides have considerable incentive to refrain from involvement in interstate disputes; this, in fact, has been recognized by Moscow and Washington during the Iran-Iraq War. Although there has been some evidence of Soviet support for Iran and at least an attempt by President Saddam Hussein to build a closer relationship with the United States,[182] both superpowers have remained in the background during this conflict. Some have suggested that principles of conflict management and a "shared definition of what constitutes behavior by outside powers in the region" might be an appropriate starting point for reducing superpower tensions in the region.[183] Such notions, however, should be greeted with some skepticism, since they assume a considerable convergence of strategic interests in the region between the two superpowers, which is clearly absent.

It is unlikely that the United States will be able to negotiate agreements with *enough* states in the gulf to allow large numbers of U.S. troops and equipment to deploy ashore during a crisis. Certainly, additional prepositioning of material can be negotiated for, as well as minimal assurances that certain facilities will be available during very specific sets of circumstances. To be sure, such agreements most probably will not operate during a crisis. If a host nation finds its sovereignty and territorial integrity greatly endangered, the presence of U.S. troops may prove quite attractive. Nevertheless, prudent strategic planning dictates that such arrangements be preplanned.

An Allied Contingency Force

A significant naval presence deployed just "over the horizon" might act as a deterrent to Soviet intervention and perhaps even internal revolt. U.S. carrier battle groups equipped with marine amphibious units would be able to arrive in a timely fashion if stationed in the region, assuming some strategic warning. A deterrent strategy, however, ought to recognize the large stake that European and Japanese allies of the United States have in the security of Persian Gulf oil. Indeed, their dependence on gulf crude far exceeds U.S. dependence. Consequently, serious consideration should be given to the creation of an allied command (outside the NATO framework) committed to contingencies arising in Southwest Asia and the Persian Gulf region. This allied contingency force would be similar in conception to the NATO ACE Mobile Force (AMF) that was developed to respond to crises on NATO's flanks. It would draw its strength from those NATO powers whose interests in Persian Gulf stability are particularly acute. Its membership might include Italian, French, U.S., German, and British forces with air, ground, and naval components. The U.S. Navy should not be expected to bear the full burden of gulf security. In fact, certain allies (the French and Italians, for example, already have considerable naval forces operating in the Indian Ocean area). The Italians have recently deployed their first aircraft carrier, the *Garibaldi*, in the Mediterranean. In addition, to ensure that the Alliance seriously addresses the value of the gulf to the West, NATO should institutionalize a political consultative mechanism to deal with questions of gulf security. Such a group has already been suggested by several prominent European security experts.[184]

A Role for Turkey

Finally, NATO should broaden its strategic perspective to provide roles for Alliance states whose geographic position allows unique contributions to both Europe and the Middle East. Turkey is the prime example. Its ties to the Islamic and Arab worlds, unique within NATO, would allow the Turkish government to assume a most valuable political and military role during any crisis in the gulf region. There are, however, obvious limits to Turkey's contribution because of rather strong historical sensitivities. Nevertheless, Turkey is potentially the most valuable Western ally in any gulf contingency. Its position on the border of the Soviet Union allows the employment of tactical aircraft (particularly from eastern

Turkey) for the interdiction of Soviet air operations as well as target coverage of proximate parts of the gulf. Deployment of forces to the gulf from bases in eastern Turkey would provide optimal projection capability, short of a Western combat presence in the gulf itself, which is not in prospect. Finally, Turkey would be an ideal location for an allied contingency force headquarters.

That the Persian Gulf is vital to Western interests ought to be axiomatic. Politically, economically, and militarily, the gulf must continue to figure prominently in both U.S. and NATO strategy for the future. There is every indication that it will continue to be a high priority in the Soviet strategic calculus. Its unique internal complexities, which include historically rooted conflicts of ideology, religion, and territory, demand attention that is sensitive to the synergistic relationship between indigenous conflict and the potential for external exploitation of internal stresses for strategic gain. Western interest will be maintained only if the West is willing to invest in the security of the region.

CONCLUSION

For much of the last thirty-five years East-West relations have been defined largely in terms of the Warsaw Pact threat to central Europe and corresponding NATO efforts to construct a credible defensive strategy to counter this threat. Consequently, regions outside of the central front but within NATO have been regarded as less vulnerable to Soviet political or military probes and, therefore, peripheral to the primary mission of defending the center. However, Soviet adventurism on NATO's southern "fringe"—the southern flank and the Persian Gulf/Middle East—makes it clear that the Western security agenda must be broadened to acknowledge potential strategic shifts in Soviet security policy as well as political shifts within NATO.

Soviet ability to exploit the serious gaps in NATO's defensive shield on the southern flank makes it urgent that the Alliance adopt a series of corrective programs to strengthen its position in the region. In addressing the issues, one key reality must be acknowledged: that NATO's capacity to reverse the political and military decline of the southern region has decreased as regional vulnerabilities and strategic importance have increased. A determination must be made as to the seriousness of the decline in the larger context of NATO's security priorities. Clearly, other regions will compete for Western resources, and there will continue to be great pressures on NATO governments to increase their respective contributions to NATO. Nevertheless, the comparative strategic decline of the southern flank and the increased Soviet military presence there *should* translate into a key priority for Alliance attention.

The two major weaknesses in the southern region are: (1) a lack of strategic partnership among the five NATO flank nations, which threatens the Alliance's political-military structure in the Mediterranean, and (2) the erosion of NATO's regional military capability in the south. The first weakness will be the more difficult one to manage, since it involves the resolution of a historically rooted interstate dispute. Without a greater commitment by the NATO council to arbitrate the serious political-military problems that flow from the Greek-Turkish feud (such as command and control in the Aegean) there is little hope for a settlement. Since the two countries have been hesitant to negotiate directly, a third party must be introduced; the NATO secretary general would be an ideal candidate for that role.

The second weakness will be reversed only if there is an Alliance-wide effort to create a funding pool through a multilateral NATO program to which all the allies contribute proportionately. To this end NATO should create a southern flank strategic requirements program to investigate the region's military modernization needs. This would be structurally similar to the 1979 NATO Long-Term Defense Program, which recognized the political necessity to involve all of the allies. Issues of southern flank readiness affect the entire Alliance and, therefore, the corrective measures must be Alliance-wide. There could also be a significant political benefit from a strategic requirements program. An Alliance-wide effort to bolster NATO's position in the Mediterranean might force the allies to recognize that the flanks cannot be regarded as appendages, strategically detached from the central front.

Efforts to broaden NATO's strategic horizon to include the Persian Gulf will be exceedingly difficult for a number of reasons. The Persian Gulf lies outside NATO's formal treaty boundary, and while clearly pressing strategic needs exist within that boundary, these are being ignored. Nevertheless, there are ways in which NATO nations can act without the formal Alliance imprimatur. One alternative would be the creation of an allied contingency force, which would be similar in conception to the ACE Mobile Force (AMF) developed to respond to crises on NATO's flanks. The allied contingency force, drawing its strength from those NATO powers whose interests are directly at risk in the gulf, would be independent of NATO authority and, therefore, free of the political obstacles that could hobble rapid response to a deteriorating "out-of-area" crisis. An East-West crisis in the Middle East becomes more likely as the Soviet Union increases its presence with radical states in the region, particularly with Libya and Syria.

The arguments presented in this study should not be regarded as a rejection of the necessity to continue investing in the credibility of a deterrent designed to protect central Europe. Rather, it is a plea to modernize Western concepts of conflict to encompass regions that may be emerging as targets for Alliance adversaries. The NATO charter may limit NATO's defensive responsibilities to a defined geographic area, but that limitation is artificial and reflective of an earlier age when the Western deterrent was unquestioned and Soviet capabilities to challenge that deterrent were limited. Today the Soviet Union is a global power with unquestioned capabilities to project military force beyond central Europe to regions whose strategic value might, tragically, be realized only after they are lost. The Soviets have already demonstrated a more aggressive projection strategy with the 1979 invasion of Afghanistan and a persistent naval buildup in the Mediterranean Sea and Indian Ocean. Further, Moscow's search for vulnerable political seams in the fabric of the Alliance has led Soviet leaders to explore bilateral relationships with fringe nations—such as Greece—whose allegiance to NATO has wavered.

History is replete with examples of strategic opportunities missed or ignored. More often than not these resulted from a desperate clinging to threadbare strategies overtaken by the inevitable evolution of international politics. An alliance founded upon the voluntary contributions of its members to a collective deterrent can ill afford to pursue a strategy that assumes the infinite capability to deter, without a continuing commitment to examine periodically the strategic credibility of the deterrent. The consequences could be tragic if the incentive for such an examination came only as the result of a Soviet test of that strategy.

NOTES

Chapter 1

1. General T.R. Milton, USAF (Ret.), "NATO's Troubled Southern Flank," *Strategic Review*, vol. 3, no. 4 (Fall 1975), 30.

2. Sir Peter Hill Norton, *No Soft Options: The Politico–Military Realities of NATO* (Toronto: McGill-Queens University Press, 1978), 72.

3. George Blanchard, Isaac Kidd, and John W. Vogt, "Problems of Readiness, Reinforcement, and Resupply," in Kenneth Rush, Brent Scowcroft, and Joseph Wolf, eds., *Strengthening Deterrence: NATO and the Credibility of Western Defense in the 1980's* (New York: Ballinger, 1978), 152–53.

4. *NATO and the Warsaw Pact: Force Comparisons* (Brussels: NATO Information Service, June 1984).

5. For a discussion of the possible economic impact on the West of another oil crisis, see Walter Goldstein, "Economic Nationalism and the Disruption of World Trade: The Impact of the Third Oil Shock," in Robert Lieber, ed., *Will Europe Fight for Oil?* (New York: Praeger, 1983), 174.

6. Harold Brown, *Thinking About National Security* (Boulder, Colo.: Westview Press, 1983), 142.

7. Pierre Hassner, "Détente and the Politics of Instability in Southern Europe" in Uwe Nerlich and Johan Holst, eds., *Beyond Nuclear Deterrence* (New York: Crane Russak, 1977), 41–59.

Chapter 2

8. Although Spain was admitted into NATO in May 1982, its forces have not been integrated into the Alliance's military structure.

9. Admiral Harold E. Shear, "The Southern Flank of NATO," *NATO's Fifteen Nations*, vol. 23, no. 6 (December/January 1979), 19.

10. From author's discussions with U.S. government officials and AFSOUTH staff.

11. Admiral William J. Crowe, Jr., "Allied Defense of the Southern Region," *NATO's Sixteen Nations*, vol. 28, no. 3 (May/June 1983), 20.

Chapter 3

12. From author's discussions with AFSOUTH staff; also see the FY 1987 JCS Posture Statement, which lists current U.S. naval deployments in the Mediterranean as "1 or 2 carrier battle groups." See *U.S. Military Posture, FY 1986* (Organization of the Joint Chiefs of Staff), 1984, 38.

13. John Marriott, "The Balance of Power in the Mediterranean," *Armed Forces Journal* (May 17, 1971), 34.

14. For McNamara's views, see Senate Committee on Armed Services, subcommittee on defense appropriations, *"Part I Department of Defense Appropriations, 1965"* (Washington, D.C.: GPO, 1964), 124.

15. See James R. Schlesinger, *Annual Defense Department Report, FY 1976*, U.S. Department of Defense (February 1975), III-27.

16. Admiral Horatio Rivero, "Why a U.S. Fleet in the Mediterranean?" *U.S. Naval Institute Proceedings, Naval Review, 1977*, vol. 103, no. 391 (May 1977), 88.

17. For a discussion of Soviet naval strategy and possible Western responses, see Paul H. Nitze and Leonard Sullivan, *Securing the Seas* (Boulder, Colo.: Westview Press, 1979), 142.

18. For the text of the Montreux Convention, see Manley O. Hudson, ed., "Convention Concerning the Regime of the Straits, Signed at Montreux, July 20, 1936," *International Legislation, 1935–1937*, vol. 7 (Washington, D.C.: Carnegie Endowment for International Peace), 386–404.

19. Admiral Nejat Tumer, "Naval Control of the Turkish Straits," *NATO's Fifteen Nations*, Special Issue 2 (1982), 86.

20. Norman Polmar, *Guide to the Soviet Navy*, 3d ed. (Annapolis, Md.: Naval Institute Press, 1983), 19.

21. Robert E. Harkavy, *Great Power Competition for Overseas Bases: The Geopolitics of Access Diplomacy* (New York: Pergamon, 1982), 186.

22. The Israeli reports were privately confirmed to the author by U.S. officials.

23. From author's discussions with U.S. government officials.

24. Bradford Dismukes and James McConnell, eds., *Soviet Naval Diplomacy* (New York: Pergamon, 1979), 168.

25. Ibid., 171.

26. Admiral Elmo Zumwalt, Jr., *On Watch* (New York: Quadrangle Books, 1976), 293.

27. Ibid., 297.

28. The process by which U.S. military forces are placed on alert is the Defense Condition (DEFCON) system. There are five levels of DEFCON readiness, the details of which are highly classified. In peacetime U.S. forces are normally at DEFCON V. The DEFCON III condition has seldom been instituted and is reserved for situations in which a mid-level alert of U.S. forces is deemed

necessary on the basis of conditions surrounding an evolving crisis. For example, components of U.S. forces were at DEFCON III status (or higher) during the 1973 Arab-Israeli War and the Cuban missile crisis.

Chapter 4

29. Data for this section are taken from a number of sources, including John M. Collins, *U.S.-Soviet Military Balance, 1980–1985* (New York: Pergamon Brasseys, 1985); *The Military Balance, 1984–1985, 1985–1986* (London: International Institute for Strategic Studies, 1984, 1985); *NATO and the Warsaw Pact: Force Comparisons* (Brussels: NATO Information Service, 1984); interviews with U.S. government officials and AFSOUTH staff.

30. These figures are taken from *Report on Allied Contributions to the Common Defense* (U.S. Department of Defense, March 1985).

31. For a discussion of Italy's role in NATO, see Raimondo Luraghi, "The Italian Role in NATO," in Lawrence Kaplan et al., eds., *NATO and the Mediterranean* (Wilmington, Del.: Scholarly Resources, 1985).

32. For a discussion of this, see Ivan Volgyes, *The Political Reliability of the Warsaw Pact Armies* (Durham, N.C.: Duke University Press, 1982).

33. Andriana Ierodiaconou, "Greece Seen Taking AWACS," *Washington Post*, Oct. 1, 1984, A–15.

Chapter 5

34. See George Harris, *Troubled Alliance: Turkish-American Problems in Historical Perspective, 1945–1971* (Washington, D.C.: American Enterprise Institute, 1972), 66–68.

35. *Documents on International Affairs, 1960* (London: Oxford University Press, 1964), 419–21.

36. Kh. Grigoryan, "Effects of Turkey's Militarization," *International Affairs* (Moscow), no. 1 (January 1960), 77.

37. Cited in Alvin Z. Rubinstein, *Soviet Policy Toward Turkey, Iran, and Afghanistan: The Dynamics of Influence* (New York: Praeger, 1982), 14.

38. L. Suyetina, "Turkey: 'Atlantic' and National Interests," *International Affairs* (Moscow), no. 7 (July 1980), 117.

39. Michael M. Boll, "Turkey's New National Security Concept: What It Means for NATO," *Orbis* (Fall 1979), 622.

40. Rubinstein, 41.

41. For an excellent discussion of this, see Paul Henze, "The Long Effort to Destabilize Turkey," *Wall Street Journal*, Oct. 7, 1981.

42. Rubinstein, 14.

43. The text of the Johnson letter was reprinted in the *Middle East Journal* (Summer 1966), 386–89.

44. Ibid.

45. See Bülent Ecevit's address reprinted in the September/October 1978 issue of *Survival* (London: International Institute for Strategic Studies, 1978).

46. Curt Gasteyger, "The Southern Flank: New Dimensions for the Alliance" in Kenneth Myers, ed., *NATO: The Next Thirty Years* (Boulder, Colo.: Westview Press, 1980), 181.

47. *United States–West European Relations in 1980.* Hearings before the subcommittee on Europe and the Middle East of the House Committee on Foreign Affairs, 96th Cong., 2d sess. (Washington, D.C.: GPO, 1980), 168–69.

48. Marvin Howe, "Turks Will Form First Civilian Cabinet Since 1980," *New York Times*, Dec. 18, 1983, A–15.

49. "New Leader Sees Turkey as West's Bridge to Mideast," *Washington Post*, Dec. 16, 1983, E–4.

50. *The Defense and Economic Cooperation Agreement—U.S. Interests and Turkish Needs.* Report of the Comptroller General of the United States, U.S. General Accounting Office, May 1982, ID–82–31 (Washington, D.C.: GPO, 1982), 31–39.

51. Reported in Foreign Broadcast Information Service (FBIS), Western Europe, Nov. 22, 1982, T–3.

52. Ibid., Nov. 30, 1982, T–1.

53. "U.S. Will Assist Turkey In Improving Air Defense," *Aviation Week & Space Technology* (Feb. 20, 1984), 68–70.

Chapter 6

54. *Turkey, Greece and NATO: The Strained Alliance.* A staff report to the Senate Committee on Foreign Relations (March 1980), 59.

55. Marian Kirsch Leighton, *Greco-Turkish Friction: Changing Balance in the Mediterranean*, Conflict Studies, no. 109 (London: The Institute for the Study of Conflict, July 1979), 6.

56. Ibid.

57. Andriana Ierodiaconou, "Greece Quits NATO Exercise in Island Dispute with Turks," *Washington Post*, Sept. 1983.

58. Ibid.

59. "Greece Refuses to Join in NATO Maneuvers," *New York Times*, Mar. 6, 1983, 21.

60. FBIS, Western Europe, Nov. 30, 1982, S–1.

61. "Greece Refuses to Join in NATO Maneuvers."

62. Barnaby J. Feder, "Britain Asks Consultations on Cyprus," *New York Times*, Nov. 16, 1983, A–18.

63. Marvin Howe, "Turks Recognize the New Nation," *New York Times*, Nov. 16, 1983, A–18.

64. Don Oberdorfer, "Turkish Move in Cyprus Criticized," *Washington Post*, Apr. 19, 1984, A–35.

65. Marvin Howe, "Rival Cypriot Leaders Meet at U.N. to Seek Final Pact," *New York Times*, Jan. 18, 1985, A–3.

66. Henry Kamm, "Greek Cypriot is Called Cool to the Latest UN Unity Plan," *New York Times*, Apr. 17, 1986, A–10.

Chapter 7

67. Andriana Ierodiaconou, "Soviet-Greek Declaration Endorses European Nuclear-Free Zone," *Washington Post*, Feb. 25, 1983, A–15.

68. Marvin Howe, "Greece Joins Soviet in Urging Deep Arms Cuts," *New York Times*, Feb. 25, 1983, A–3.

69. Ibid.

70. Dan Morgan, "U.S. Plans Sharp Rise in Military Aid to Turkey," *Washington Post*, Feb. 5, 1983, A–11.

71. FBIS, Western Europe, Feb. 7, 1983, S–2.

72. Robert W. Komer, "Aid to Greece and Turkey: The 70% Solution," *Wall Street Journal*, Apr. 5, 1983, 30.

73. Ibid.

74. *Congressional Presentation for Security Assistance Programs FY 1987* (2 vols.) (Washington, D.C.: U.S. Department of State, 1986).

75. F. Stephen Larrabee, "Greece for the Greeks," *Foreign Policy*, no. 45, Winter 1981–82, 170.

76. "Talks on Bases in Greece Resume as Tensions Rise," *New York Times*, Mar. 20, 1983, 8.

77. Marvin Howe, "U.S. and Greece at Odds on Landings at Crete Base," *New York Times*, Jan. 13, 1983, 6.

78. Paul Anatasi, "Greece Drops Protest on Turkish Shelling," *New York Times*, Mar. 10, 1984, 3.

79. Fred Hiatt, "Weinberger Poses Greek Base Deal," *Washington Post*, Mar. 31, 1984, A–19.

Chapter 8

80. Tom Burns, "Spanish Communists under Coroner's Knife," *Washington Post*, Mar. 20, 1983, A–19.

81. Tom Burns, "Spaniards Vote to Remain in NATO," *Washington Post*, Mar. 13, 1986, 1.

82. For an excellent discussion of these internal factors, see Gregory Treverton, "Spain: Domestic Politics and Security Policy," *Adelphi Papers*, no. 204 (London: International Institute for Strategic Studies, Spring 1986).

83. *Military Balance, 1985–1986*, 56.

84. Interviews with State Department officials confirm that the Spanish had raised the issue of nuclear overflight in connection with negotiations over levels of U.S. military aid for Spain.

85. Michael Getler, "Visiting Minister Says U.S. Accords Shortchange Spain," *Washington Post*, Mar. 14, 1984, A–18.

Opportunities Missed

86. See *Greece and Turkey: Some Military Implications Related to NATO and the Middle East.* Prepared for the special subcommittee on investigations of the

House Committee on Foreign Affairs by the Congressional Research Service (February 1975), 16.

Chapter 9

87. U.S. House of Representatives, subcommittee on Europe and the Middle East, Hearings on *NATO After Afghanistan,* 96th Cong., 2d sess., 1980, 7.

88. See *Department of State Bulletin,* February 1980, for text of the address.

89. Zbigniew Brzezinski, *Power and Principle: Memoirs of the National Security Advisor, 1977–1981* (New York: Farrar, Straus, Giroux, 1983), 478. Also see the memoirs of former secretary of state Cyrus Vance, *Hard Choices* (New York: Simon & Schuster, 1983), 384–97, and the brief discussion of the Afghanistan invasion in Gary Sick, *All Fall Down* (New York: Random House, 1985), 247–49.

90. Quoted in *New York Times,* Jan. 1, 1980, 1.

91. The *New York Times,* Dec. 12, 1980, reported that in the first nine months after the Soviet invasion of Afghanistan the Federal Republic of Germany increased its trade with the Soviet Union by 31 percent.

Chapter 10

92. Bruce R. Kuniholm, *The Origins of the Cold War in the Near East* (Princeton, N.J.: Princeton University Press, 1980).

93. Ibid., 201.

94. Brzezinski, 369.

95. Quoted in Alvin Z. Rubinstein, *Soviet Policy Toward Turkey, Iran, and Afghanistan: The Dynamics of Influence* (New York: Praeger, 1982), 66.

96. J.C. Hurewitz, "The Interplay of Superpower and Regional Dynamics," in Mark V. Kauppi and R. Craig Nation, eds., *The Soviet Union and the Middle East in the 1980s* (Lexington, Mass.: Lexington Books, 1983), 20.

97. *Public Papers of the Presidents of the United States, Dwight David Eisenhower, 1957* (Washington, D.C.: National Archives and Records Service, GPO, 1958), 13.

98. Mohammed Heikal, *The Sphinx and the Commissar: The Rise and Fall of Soviet Influence in the Middle East* (New York: Harper & Row, 1978), 74.

99. Peter Mansfield, ed., *The Middle East: A Political and Economic Survey* (Oxford: Oxford University Press, 1980), 34.

100. B.H. Liddell Hart, *Defense of the West* (London: Cassell, 1950), 245.

101. See, for example, the discussion by former British prime minister Harold Macmillan in vol. 3 of his memoirs, *Tides of Fortune 1945–1955* (London: Harper & Row, 1969), 573.

102. British forces in Malta and Cyprus were key elements of the Suez invasion force. See Gregory Blaxland, *The Regiments Depart* (London: William Klimber, 1971), 236–60.

103. Jacob Abadi, *Britain's Withdrawal from the Middle East, 1947–1971: The Economic and Strategic Imperatives* (Princeton, N.J.: The Kingston Press, Inc., 1982), 198.

104. *Times* (London), Aug. 3, 1965, also quoted in Abadi, 203.

105. J.B. Kelly, *Arabia, the Gulf and the West* (New York: Basic Books, 1980), 57–58.

106. D.C. Watt, "The Decision to Withdraw," *Political Quarterly*, vol. 34, no. 3, 310.

107. Richard M. Nixon, "Asia After Vietnam," *Foreign Affairs*, vol. 46, no. 1 (October 1967), 114.

108. *Public Papers of the Presidents of the United States, Richard Milhous Nixon, 1970* (Washington, D.C.: National Archives and Records Service, GPO, 1971), 549.

109. Ibid., 903.

110. Ibid., 906.

111. Ibid., 118–19.

112. Ibid., 154.

113. Ibid., 748.

114. Shahram Chubin, *Security in the Persian Gulf: The Role of Outside Powers* (London: Allanheld, Osmun, 1982, for the International Institute for Strategic Studies), 11.

115. Data obtained from the Defense Security Assistance Agency, U.S. Department of Defense.

116. See, for example, Lewis Sorley, *Arms Transfers Under Nixon: A Policy Analysis* (Lexington, Ky.: University Press of Kentucky, 1983), 44–45.

117. See, for example, Chubin, 11.

118. Richard M. Nixon, *RN: The Memoirs of Richard Nixon* (New York: Grosset & Dunlap, 1978), 481.

119. Lawrence Whetton, "The Arab-Israeli Dispute: Great Power Behavior," *Adelphi Papers*, no. 128 (London: International Institute for Strategic Studies, Winter 1976/1977), 17.

120. *Great Power Competition for Overseas Bases*, 188.

121. Robert O. Freedman, "The Soviet Union and Sadat's Egypt," in Michael MccGuire et al., *Soviet Naval Policy* (New York: Praeger, 1975).

122. Quoted in Edward Sheehan, *The Arabs, Israel and Kissinger* (New York: Readers Digest Press, 1976), 22.

123. A notable exception is the superb account of the Iranian revolution, including an analysis of the disintegration of the shah's regime, by Jerrold D. Green, *Revolution in Iran: The Politics of Countermobilization* (New York: Praeger, 1982).

Chapter 11

124. For the text of the GCC Charter, see *The Gulf Cooperation Council* (Riyadh: GCC Secretariat, 1982).

125. *Middle East Economic Digest*, Oct. 28, 1983, 23.

126. See *Congressional Presentation for Security Assistance Programs*, Fiscal Year 1987, vol. 1 (Washington, D.C.: U.S. Department of State, 1986), 99.

127. Obviously, neither Oman nor Turkey could assume Saudi Arabia's place in the Middle East strategic landscape. But, if Saudi Arabia refuses to accept a role consonant with its position as the largest foreign military sales recipient, it is only prudent for the United States to seek a *combination* of states that could at least assume some of the strategic burden that the Saudis refuse to carry.

128. *Strategic Survey, 1984–85* (London: International Institute for Strategic Studies, 1985), 68.

129. John Duke Anthony, "The Gulf Cooperation Council," *Journal of South-Asian and Middle Eastern Studies*, vol. 5, no. 4 (Summer 1982), 15.

130. From author's discussions with U.S. officials.

131. *Joint Publication Review Service* (JPRS) vol. 49, no. 6, Dec. 20, 1983, 6.

132. Data for this section are drawn from a variety of sources, including *Military Balance, 1984–1985, 1985–1986, Aviation Week & Space Technology* (1985–1986), and Anthony Cordesman, *The Gulf and the Search for Strategic Stability* (Boulder, Colo.: Westview Press, 1984).

133. Cordesman, 489.

134. *World Military Expenditures and Arms Transfers, 1985* (Washington, D.C.: U.S. Arms Control and Disarmament Agency, 1985), 76.

135. Ibid.

136. Ibid., 76.

137. *New York Times*, Oct. 26, 1979.

138. Paul R. Viotti, "Politics in the Yemens and the Horn of Africa: Constraints on a Superpower," in Kauppi and Nation, *The Soviet Union and the Middle East in the 1980s*, 217.

139. John Kifner, "Battle for Southern Yemen: How the Fury Began," *New York Times*, Jan. 30, 1986, A–4.

140. *Military Balance*, 82.

141. Anthony Cordesman, "Oman: The Guardian of the Eastern Gulf," *Armed Forces Journal International* (June 1983), 29.

142. *Middle East Economic Digest*, May 18, 1984, 1.

143. From author's discussions with U.S. officials.

Chapter 12

144. See Francis Fukuyama, "Nuclear Shadowboxing: Soviet Intervention in the Middle East," *Orbis*, vol. 25, no. 3 (Fall 1981), 580.

145. See Shahram Chubin, "U.S. Security Interests in the Persian Gulf in the 1980s," *Daedalus* (Fall 1980), 47–48.

146. Shahram Chubin, "The Soviet Union and Iran," *Foreign Affairs*, vol. 61, no. 4 (Spring 1983), 934.

147. Ibid., 939.

148. Dennis Ross, "Considering Soviet Threats to the Persian Gulf," *International Security*, vol. 6, no. 2 (Fall 1981), 168.

149. The Brezhnev proposal was described by a TASS commentator, Nikolai Portugalov, and was reported in Foreign Broadcast Information Service (FBIS), USSR, Mar. 3, 1980.

150. See the text of Brezhnev's proposal in FBIS, USSR, Dec. 11, 1980.

151. Data for this section are drawn from *Military Balance*, *U.S.-Soviet Military Balance, 1980–1985*, and *Force Structure Summary: USSR, Eastern Europe, and Mongolia* (unclassified), Defense Intelligence Agency, DDB-2680-170A-85, November 1985.

152. Soviet naval activity is discussed in Part 1 of this study.

153. *Military Balance*, 28.

154. Congressional Budget Office, *U.S. Ground Forces: Design and Cost Alternatives for NATO and Non-NATO Contingencies*, December 1980, 49–50.

155. James P. Roche, "Projection of Military Power to Southwest Asia: An Asymmetrical Problem" in Ra'anan, 219.

156. Henry S. Bradsher, *Afghanistan and the Soviet Union* (Chapel Hill, N.C.: Duke University Press, 1983), 206.

157. See U.S. Department of State, *Chemical Warfare in Southeast Asia and Afghanistan*, Special Report no. 98, 1982.

158. Roche, 219–20.

159. One analyst has suggested, for example, that the Soviet Union might limit a military campaign to northwestern Iran. See Thomas L. McNaugher, *Arms and Oil: U.S. Military Strategy in the Persian Gulf* (Washington, D.C.: The Brookings Institution, 1985), 46.

160. Caspar W. Weinberger, *Annual Report to the Congress, Fiscal Year 1985* (Washington, D.C.: GPO, 1984). (Hereafter referred to as "FY 1985 Posture Statement.")

161. Ibid., 39.

162. Caspar W. Weinberger, *Annual Report to the Congress, Fiscal Year 1984* (Washington, D.C.: GPO, 1983), 17. (Hereafter referred to as "FY 1984 Posture Statement.")

163. FY 1985 Posture Statement, 40.

164. During a period of service in the Department of State (1981–82) the author observed that, when "clearing" such documents with other agencies, the department was not always successful in persuading the Pentagon to distinguish between objectives for the two regions.

165. Prepared statement of the Honorable Nicholas A. Veliotes, assistant secretary of state for Near East and South Asian affairs, U.S. Department of State, in *U.S. Policy Toward the Persian Gulf.* Joint hearings before the subcommittee on Europe and the Middle East of the Senate Foreign Relations Committee and Joint Economic Committee, House of Representatives, 97th Cong., 2d sess., May 10, 1982, 6.

166. Ibid., 8.

167. Ibid., 9.

168. George Wilson and David Hoffman, "U.S. Ends Naval Exercises Off Libya," *Washington Post*, Mar. 28, 1986, 1.

169. Ihsan Hijazi, "Libyan-Soviet Ties Reported Strained," *New York Times*, May 6, 1986, A–3.

170. Statement by the Honorable Francis J. West, Jr., assistant secretary of defense for international security affairs, on *Defense Policy for Southwest Asia*

and the Rapid Deployment Force, before the subcommittee on seapower and force projection of the Senate Armed Services Committee, 97th Cong., 2d sess., Mar. 12, 1982, 1.

171. Ibid.

172. FY 1984 Posture Statement, 192.

173. Ibid., 198–99.

174. Caspar W. Weinberger, *Annual Report to the Congress, Fiscal Year 1986* (Washington, D.C.: GPO, 1985), 200.

175. Ibid., 204.

176. Ibid., 196.

177. See Albert Wohlstetter, "Half-Wars and Half-Policies in the Persian Gulf," in W. Scott Thompson, ed., *National Security in the 1980's: From Weakness to Strength* (San Francisco, Calif.: Institute for Contemporary Studies, 1980), 124.

178. FY 1984–FY 1987 Posture Statements.

179. Jeffrey Record, "The Rapid Deployment Force: U.S. Power Projection and the Persian Gulf," in Uri Ra'anan, Robert Pfaltzgraff, Jr., and Geoffrey Kemp, eds., *Projection of Power: Perspectives, Perceptions, and Problems* (Hamden, Conn.: Archon Books, 1982), 112.

180. U.S. Department of State, *U.S. Policy Toward the Persian Gulf,* Current Policy Document no. 390, May 1982. (Statement by Nicholas A. Veliotes, assistant secretary of state for Near East and South Asian affairs.)

181. Hearings before the House Committee on Foreign Affairs and the subcommittees on international security and scientific affairs and Europe and the Middle East, on *Proposed Sale of Airborne Warning and Control Systems (AWACS) and F–15 Enhancement to Saudi Arabia,* 97th Cong., 1st sess., September/October 1981, 39–40.

182. For a provocative discussion of Iraqi internal and foreign policy, see Christine Moss Helms, *Iraq: Eastern Flank of the Arab World* (Washington, D.C.: The Brookings Institution, 1984).

183. *Security in the Persian Gulf,* 142.

184. See Karl Kaiser, Winston Lord, Thierry de Montbrial, and David Watt, *Western Security: What Has Changed? What Should Be Done?* (New York: Council on Foreign Relations, 1981).

INDEX